Making Classic Cars in Wood

Joe B. Hicks

Sterling Publishing Co., Inc.   New York

I would like to give a special thank-you to a good friend, George Redd, who gave help and encouragement during the production of this and other books.

I dedicate this work to my son Dave. I feel that a man who has a son has a priceless treasure. Dave is a treasure to me. He is a help, an inspiration, and most of all a friend.

Library of Congress Cataloging-in-Publication Data

Hicks, Joe B.
    Making classic cars in wood / Joe B. Hicks.
        p. cm.
    ISBN 0-8069-6988-1
      1. Automobiles—Models—Design and construction.   2. Woodwork.
   I. Title.
   TL237.H49   1990
   629.22′1—dc20   89-26175
                                            CIP

Published by Sterling Publishing Co., Inc.
387 Park Avenue South, New York, N.Y. 10016
Distributed in Canada by Sterling Publishing
℅ Canadian Manda Group, P.O. Box 920, Station U
Toronto, Ontario, Canada M8Z 5P9
Distributed in Great Britain and Europe by Cassell PLC
Artillery House, Artillery Row, London SW1P 1RT, England
Distributed in Australia by Capricorn Ltd.
P.O. Box 665, Lane Cove, NSW 2066
Manufactured in the United States of America

CONTENTS

Color section follows page 64

INTRODUCTION

Since the beginning of time, man has striven to improve his mode of travel. Tired of walking and running every place he wanted to go, he learned to tame and ride wild animals. He conceived of carts and chariots, to be drawn by those animals, to provide transportation for more than one person or for carrying heavy loads. He built ships, propelled by the wind, to carry himself across the seas. He then learned to make large engines to power his chariots and ships, freeing himself from dependence on the wind and animals.

It seems that each time the human race came up with a new idea, it also started a love affair with that new form of transportation. Some of those love affairs were to last for a very long time—some extending beyond the era of practical use of the idea itself, as in the case of sailing ships and the steam-driven locomotive. We will concern ourselves with one of these love affairs in the pages of this book.

For the past century or so, much of humankind has been involved in an ongoing love affair with automobiles. For many of us, this creation of our own hands has become a very strategic and essential part of life—even to the point where we are now often helpless without it. We use this machine to transport us to our places of employment. Many of us use it while we are performing our occupations. Of course, the automobile is an important part of our domestic lives, too—of basic importance in shopping,

taking the children to school and youth activities, transporting the family to the movies on Friday night and to church on Sunday morning. It is the means by which we reach our vacation land. In some cases it has become the object of our recreation, in and of itself.

Yes, as alluded to earlier, there exists an ongoing, collective love affair that goes beyond the mere need for the services of this invention. Related to automobiles, there is a passion that takes hold of our minds and our hearts and our souls. It is this passion that drives us to make our automobiles the fastest or the prettiest or the most authentic reproductions. It is this love affair that causes us to spend countless hours in our garages—tinkering, polishing, repairing, and tuning. And it is this love affair that will not allow automobiles of the past, the ones that have outlived their practical usefulness, to die. We treat these classic cars as carefully as the new ones, even more carefully, because we understand that they are the last of their kind. When they are gone there will be no more. This book has been conceived and written so that the woodworker may now enter this nostalgic world of classic cars.

Each of the following projects has been designed so that the finished product will have enough strength to be used as a toy, yet enough detail and authenticity to be used as a display model. So wherever your interests lie along these lines, you can feel free to take them to the limit. The plans for each project have been carefully drawn to show exact shapes and dimensions. However, many of the drawings were too large for reproduction in this book in their original size; these have been reduced and superimposed upon scale grids. To enlarge these drawings back to their original size, use 1″ grid paper. Draw the original pattern in portions: one square at a time. Make the line that is to run through the 1″ grid correspond exactly to the line running through the book's smaller square. The instructions have been written so that they can be easily understood, and are supported with step-by-step photo illustrations.

You will find as you are doing these projects that your most useful bench tool will be your band saw or jigsaw. A table saw or radial arm saw will be helpful, but not essential, as will be a drill press. Hand-held tools, such as a router, finish sander, and drill motor, will make some operations faster and easier. A rotary carving tool will be handy in adding some of the detail.

Each set of instructions is preceded by a materials list to help you get started with everything you will need. A cutting list is also provided for each. The cutting list takes account of each car component by its identifying number and the quantity of that component that should be made.

Give free rein to your creative instincts as you are building and finishing these cars. Allow yourself to get involved in the detail, and the result will be some real keepsakes and collector's items.

· 1 ·
FRILLS, WHEELS, AND DETAILS

As you begin the adventure of building some of the projects of the following pages, you will inevitably reach the point where you will want to make your "Classic Car Model" look a bit more realistic. Although the plans and instructions for each project provide all the construction information you will need to build a great-looking car, the time will come when you are going to want to add a bit of detail here or express yourself with a little creative idea there. After all, these are "Classic Cars," and every detail or embellishment will only enhance the finished product. Above all, be imaginative as you are building these cars. They are your projects; I have given you only the foundation on which to build.

There are many ways to add detail to your "Classic Car." If you have a hand at carving, utilize this skill to add subtle little features that will make the car look more realistic. This is not to say that you must be a great sculptor. Often, you will need only to be able to carve a straight line into the surface of the engine hood area to create the appearance of a radiator, or add a few hash marks on a wooden seat bottom to make it look a little more like a leather seat. Then, of course, if you are really good at this sort of thing, you are at liberty to take it to the limit of your talent. You can go as far as to carve spokes into the wheels of a sports car, or instruments into the dash panel. You can use your carving talent to show the leather hood belts with their buckles, or the latches for luggage compartments. All of this fine detail is by no means necessary, but it will add authenticity and make your finished product more valuable.

For those of us, however, who are not quite so experienced or skilled with the carving tools, there are a few things we can do to add carved detail to our models. First, there are a few tools that make these little operations somewhat easier for the beginner. A simple collection of miniature files is a great help. Two or three different shapes, such as round, half-round, and three-cornered, will give you enough variety to make simple carved highlights. You may also want to try your hand with a set of carving tools from your local hardware dealer. They are not expensive, and they usually have a variety of cutting shapes to allow better control for various carving tasks. Then, of course, there is the modern approach, which I particularly like for myself, and that is the use of the rotary carving tool. These come in several styles. One type is designed so that

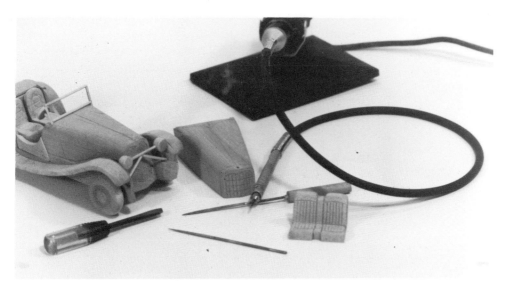

Illus. 1 Detail can be added to your "Classic Car" by using simple carving techniques.

the cutting bit is attached directly to the motor, and the motor is then held in your hand and becomes the tool handle. Another type has the motor set away on a little platform, and the tool's cutting bit, then, is driven by a flexible shaft that is generally two or three feet long. Each type has its advantages. The flexible shaft type has the advantage that there is going to be a smaller, more easily handled tool in your hand. It has the disadvantage of shaft maintenance. Due to the high speed capability of the motor, the shaft can become quite hot and must be well lubricated relatively often to prevent damage to itself. The hand-held motor does not have these maintenance problems, but naturally there is more mass in your hand, and this can be a little bothersome if you are trying to master some point of fine detail.

Carving is only one way to create the finer detail you may want for your finished "Classic Car"; another, of course, is painting. I cannot say enough about the amount of detail that can be added to an otherwise simple model with the use of a few colors and a small paint brush. Most of the detail one could add by carving can be achieved by painting, as well. For instance, we mentioned the radiator detail while discussing the carving technique. Well, one could easily set the radiator area of the hood apart by painting it a different color, such as chrome or brass. The spokes of a sports car wheel can be designated on a solid wooden wheel by painting the entire wheel flat black and then adding the spokes with a small brush and some chrome model paint. Those dash instruments can be created in much the same way. You can designate leather seats simply by choosing the proper color when painting the wood corresponding to the seats. Painting has one major advantage over carving in that if you are not pleased with the outcome, you can do the job again without damage to the part in question. A little forethought during the construction of the project can help in the painting of detail: think about how you want various parts to look and how you are going to paint them prior to assembly. This will make it easier for you to get your paint brushes into otherwise hard-to-get spots, and will allow for better control of the brush. You may want to employ both carving and painting while detailing your finished models.

The careful shaping of some of the major parts during the construction process can do much to enhance the finished appearance of your projects. For example, rounding the tops of fenders of old roadsters or radiusing the corners of the engine hood area or other body areas can add authenticity to many of your projects.

A more realistic model can sometimes be created by the addition of the right kind of wheels. Some of the older cars should have spoked wheels, which gives them the feel of the era that their designs specify. Most cars of the 1930s, 1940s, and 1950s should have solid wheels with rounded features, to advance the appearance of hubcaps and rubber tires. Both types of wheel are generally available from woodworkers' supply houses. The more modern cars, however, should have wider tires with somewhat square outside corners, to designate the new low-profile tires of today. Toy wheels of this variety are not available and must be made in your workshop.

The art of making wheels is not a difficult thing to master; however, it is a bit time-consuming, primarily because you generally need quite a few for each project. I usually set aside one afternoon for the purpose of making wheels for my ongoing projects, and do them all at one time.

I recommend the use of maple for the production of wooden wheels, because it is a tough wood and can stand up to the treatment it will receive in the production process, to say nothing of that it will receive by virtue of its being part of a child's toy.

To create your own wooden wheel design, first select the wheel's outer diameter, according to the needs of the project. It is good to give yourself a range of sizes, such as 1½″ to 1¾″. The wheel will be cut with a hole saw and the precise size may not be attainable. Many of the projects within this book use wheels of approximately 1½″ diameter; therefore, let's go through the steps for making a wheel of that size. The thickness of the material used to make the wheel will be the finished width of the wheel. This should be taken into consideration during selection of the material. Most of our projects will look good with wheels of approximately ¾″ width, so we can select a common ¾″ hardwood stock material. Hardwood material is usually milled to an actual thickness of ¹³⁄₁₆″, however, but that will not be a major problem for us. Now, we must draw a circle of 1½″ diameter to begin the actual layout of our wheel design. Mark the center of the circle; this will become important shortly, as you can imagine.

Next, draw a circle ⅞″ in diameter inside the first. This will indicate where tire and wheel come together. If you choose to add detail within the wheel, such as small holes to give the appearance of racing-type mag wheels, or possibly a couple of rings to give the appearance of a modern hubcap, then you should draw smaller circles to locate where these things will happen. Note the design for our wheel in Illus. 2. We will drill five small holes to make a racing-type mag wheel design. That is why this illustration has the five equally spaced lines radiating from the center—to indicate the location of these five holes. By the way, to space five such lines on a circle there must be

Illus. 2   Layout for a wheel on ¾″ hardwood stock.

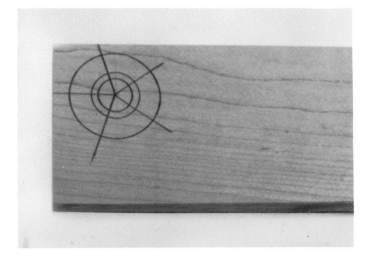

Illus. 3   Drilling holes around the center of the wheel gives the appearance of a mag wheel.

Illus. 4   Recess center portion to a depth of ⅛″.

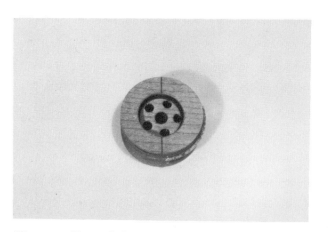

Illus. 5   Use a hole saw to relieve wheel from the flat stock.

Illus. 6   Use a drill press as a mini-lathe to shape the finished wheel.

72° between each. Illus. 3 shows the drilling of the small holes. We have chosen a hole size of 3⁄16″ diameter. Center-punching the drilling location will give better results, as maple is a hardwood and drill drift is not uncommon even if a drill press is being used.

Now, as shown in Illus. 4, we have used a ⅞″ center bore drill bit, to recess the center section of the wheel to a depth of approximately ⅛″.

Next, we will use a 1⅝″ diameter hole saw, which has approximately a 1½″ inside diameter, to relieve the entire wheel from the surrounding material (Illus. 5).

To deburr and shape the wheel, use your drill press as a sort of mini-lathe. Drill out the center hole in the wheel to ¼″ so that it will later fit a ¼″ dowel axle. Now take a ¼″ bolt, about 3 or 4″ long, and cut off the head with a hacksaw. Fit the wooden wheel on the other end (the threaded end), and secure it between two ¼″ nuts.

Illus. 7   Make several equally spaced lines to produce the appearance of tire tread.

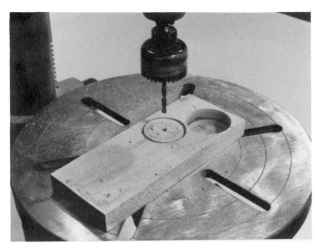

Illus. 8   Mark the next wheel with a hole saw.

Chuck the bolt into the drill press. Set the press to rotate at a medium speed, and use a wood rasp and sandpaper to clean up and bring the wheel into the desired shape (Illus. 6).

The detail of tire tread can be added in much the same way. While the wheel is still chucked up in the drill press, use a small back saw or three-corner wood rasp to mark the tread area with several equally-spaced lines, giving the appearance of tire tread (Illus. 7).

Fit the drill press once again with the hole saw, and mark another wheel by drilling slightly into the flat stock (Illus. 8). Then, drill out the center hole to ¼", and use a ¼" dowel about 2" long to pin the finished wheel to the flat stock, making it a template for drilling the 3⁄16" mag wheel holes (Illus. 9). After the first 3⁄16" hole has been drilled, another dowel of 3⁄16" diameter should be used—to prevent the template wheel from spinning during the other drilling operations.

The actual duplication of the first wheel can be repeated many times (Illus. 10), to create enough wheels for all car projects that you have immediate plans for.

As a point of interest and as something that may help you with the projects to follow, I have found that different manufacturers of toy wheels approach the design of similar wheels a bit differently. For instance, two companies may both build a 2" diameter hardwood toy wheel. One may make the wheel ½" thick and put a 3⁄16" axle hole in the center, while the other will make the thickness of the wheel ¾" and provide a ¼" hole for the axle. For this reason, note that the instructions for the projects have left the lengths and diameters of axles and the diameters of axle holes to be decided by you after you have chosen the wheels.

Several of the projects in this book have open cockpit arrangements and include a driver in place. The shaping of the driver is a simple matter. Generally, the driver can be made from dowel stock of 7⁄16" or ½" diameter. The shaping is done by cutting a section approximately 2" in length and fitting it directly into the chuck of your drill press. With the drill press running at a medium speed, use your wood rasp and sandpaper to shape the driver's head (Illus. 11).

The materials lists for many of the projects will specify hardwood block. If you find that this material is unavailable in your area, create your own hardwood block by laminating several ¾" thick pieces together, as shown in Illus. 12.

All of this said, it is now time for you to set out into the world of quality classic car building in wood. Enjoy yourself.

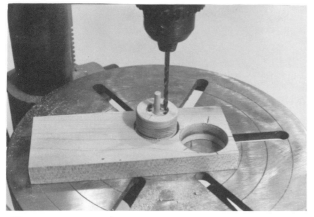

Illus. 9   Use original wheel as a drilling template.

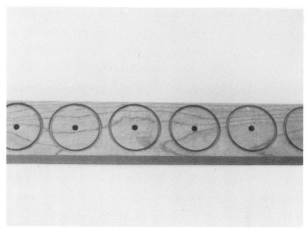

Illus. 10   Duplicate the first wheel many times.

Illus. 11   Shape the driver's head in a drill press.

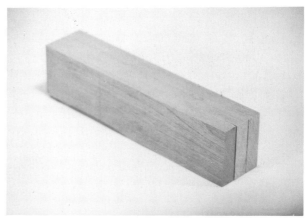

Illus. 12   Hardwood blocks can be fabricated by laminating several thinner pieces together.

· 2 ·
THE OLD TIMERS

As mentioned in the introduction, man spent eons riding on the backs of animals, and using them to pull carts and wagons. As time progressed, he was able to make his wagons nicer, prettier, and more comfortable. He applied fancy paint jobs and added upholstered seats and interiors. He provided springs for smoother rides and roofs to shield himself from the effects of bad weather. In time, the wagons became rather splendid and luxurious.

The early automobiles were not very different from the wagons that were being used at that time. They simply incorporated the necessary design changes to effect the transition from being drawn by horses to being propelled by gasoline engines.

The automobiles represented in this chapter are from this era of the horseless carriage. They are tremendous fun to build and display.

1902 Baker

Illus. 13

Materials List

Hardwood Stock, ¾" .... *3" × 20"*
Hardwood Block .... *2" × 3" × 6"*
Hardwood Dowel, ⅛" .... *20"*
Hardwood Dowel, ¼" .... *8"*
Hardwood Dowel, ⅜" .... *2"*
Spoked Hardwood Toy Wheels,
  2" diameter .... *4 each*
Carpenter's Glue .... *Small container*
Non-toxic varnish or paint of several colors in
  small containers

Cutting List

Part 1 ... *Chassis* .... *Make 1*
Part 2 ... *Body* .... *Make 1*
Part 3 ... *Body Side* .... *Make 2*
Part 4 ... *Rear Fender* .... *Make 2*
Part 5 ... *Front Fender* .... *Make 2*
Part 6 ... *Body Front* .... *Make 1*
Part 7 ... *Headlight* .... *Make 2*
Part 8 ... *Top* .... *Make 1*
Part 9 ... *Seat* .... *Make 1*

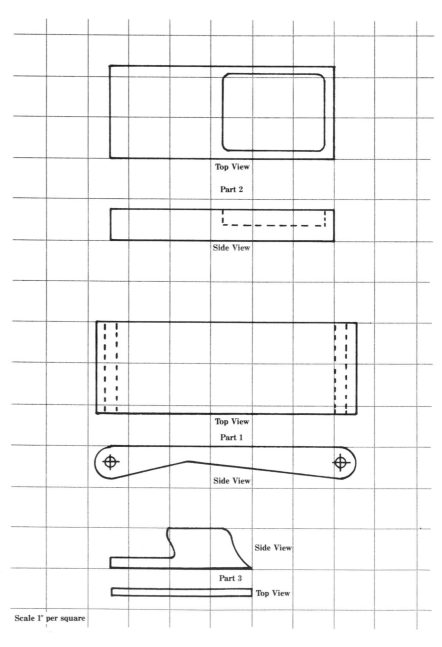

Illus. 14   Layout of parts. 1902 Baker.

Scale 1″ per square

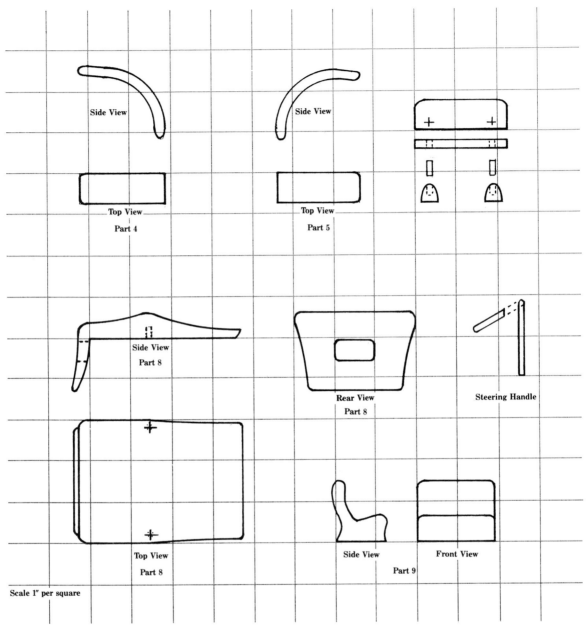

Illus. 15   Layout of parts. 1902 Baker.

Instructions

LAYOUT

1. Using ¾″ hardwood stock, lay out Parts 1 through 6. Indicate the positions for the axle holes on the car chassis (Part 1). Note that Parts 3 and 6 are not to be finished at the full thickness of the ¾″ material (Illus. 14 and 15).

2. Using a band saw or jigsaw, cut each of these parts to shape (Illus. 16).

3. Lay out the top and seat (Parts 8 and 9) on the hardwood block material (Illus. 15).

4. Use a band saw to cut these pieces to shape (Illus. 16).

5. The foot well in the body, Part 2, can be accomplished with a router. Use a straight router bit. Set a shallow depth, approximately

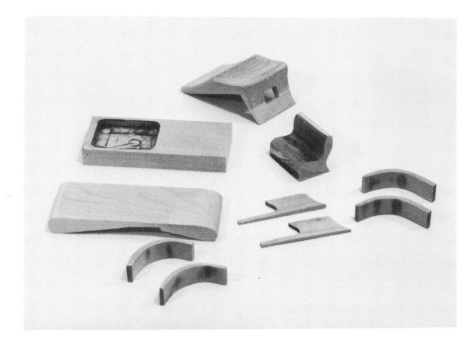

Illus. 16 Cut these parts to shape, using a band saw or jigsaw.

⅛″ or so, for your first pass; then increase the depth setting two or three times for each successive pass until you have reached the desired depth for the finished part (Illus. 14 and 16).

6. Drill the axle holes into the chassis (Part 1) (Illus. 14). The diameter of these holes will depend upon the requirements of the particular wheel that you have chosen to use.

7. The headlights (Part 7) are made from ⅜″ diameter hardwood dowel (Illus. 15). Place a short piece of the dowel in a drill press and shape it with wood rasps and sandpaper until the desired cone shape is obtained. Then cut straight across with your band saw to produce the finished headlight.

8. Sand all parts well to prepare them for final assembly. Radius corners and edges as necessary to further a realistic appearance.

ASSEMBLY

9. Align and secure the body (Part 2) to the chassis (Part 1) using carpenter's glue (Illus. 17).

10. Position and glue the seat (Part 9) in place (Illus. 17).

11. Glue the sides (Part 3) and all four fenders (Parts 4 and 5) in place (Illus. 17).

12. Drill a ⅛″ mounting hole into the body front (Part 6) and into the rear side of the headlight (Part 7), for each headlight (Illus. 15).

13. Using a short piece, ¼″ long, of ⅛″ dowel, secure each headlight into position onto the body front (Part 6) with wood glue (Illus. 15).

14. Glue the finished body front/headlight assembly into position at the front of the body (Part 2) (Illus. 17).

15. Using sections of ⅛″ dowel for vertical supports (Illus. 17), glue the top (Part 8) into position.

16. The other ⅛″ dowel top supports and braces are simply decorative. They may be glued into place at this time (Illus. 17).

17. The steering shaft and handle are made from ⅛″ dowel. They should be built up and glued into position at this time.

18. The 2″ diameter spoked wheels can be installed at this time. However, you may choose to leave them off until you have finished painting or varnishing.

19. You may now finish this 1902 Baker horseless carriage as you wish, with either non-toxic paint for a realistic look, or with varnish, to display the wood and the quality of workmanship.

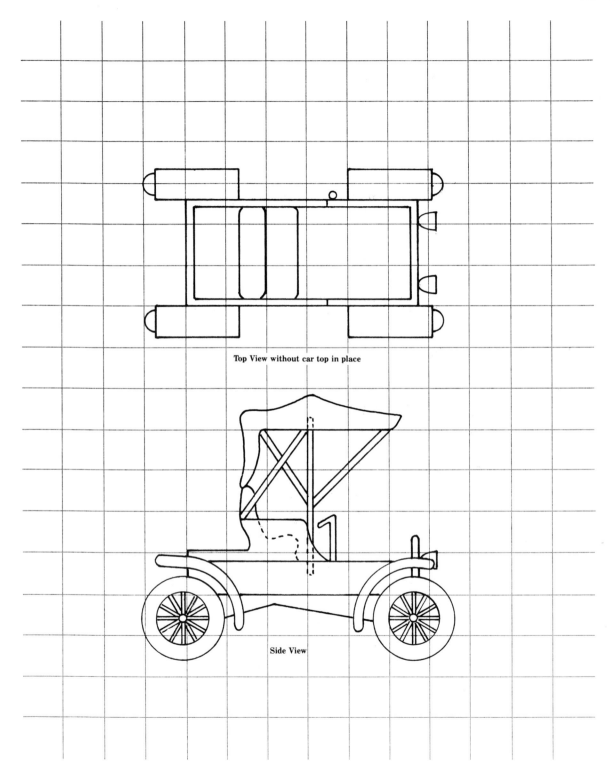

Top View without car top in place

Side View

Illus. 17   Assembled project showing parts alignment and placement.

1903 Fiat

Illus. 18

Materials List

Hardwood Stock, ¾" .... 3" × 20"

Hardwood Block .... 2" × 3" × 7"

Hardwood Dowel, ⅛" diameter .... 3"

Hardwood Dowel, ¼" diameter .... 8"

Hardwood Dowel, ⅜" diameter .... 2"

Spoked Hardwood Toy Wheels,
  2" diameter .... 4 each

Hardwood Toy Wheel, ¾" diameter ... 1 each

Carpenter's Glue .... Small container

Non-toxic paints, two or three colors in small
  containers

Cutting List

Part 1 ... Car Chassis .... Make 1

Part 2 ... Rear Floor .... Make 1

Part 3 ... Right Side Panel .... Make 1

Part 4 ... Left Side Panel .... Make 1

Part 5 ... Fire Wall .... Make 1

Part 6 ... Engine Hood .... Make 1

Part 7 ... Rear Fender .... Make 2

Part 8 ... Front Fender .... Make 2

Part 9 ... Seat .... Make 2

Part 10 .. Gearshift and Hand
              Brake .... Make 1

Part 11 .. Headlamp .... Make 2

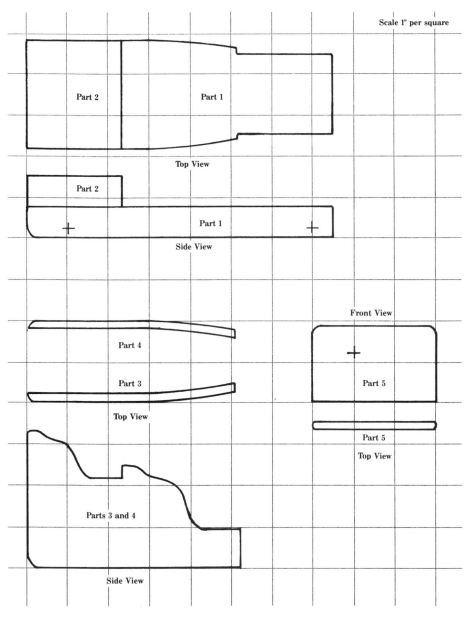

Scale 1" per square

*Illus. 19 Layout of parts.
1903 Fiat.*

Instructions

LAYOUT

1. Lay out Parts 1, 2, 3, 4, 5, 7, 8, and 10 on the ¾" hardwood material. Keep in mind that some of the parts are not a full ¾" thick and will have to be trimmed to the proper thickness (Illus. 19 and 20).

2. Lay out Parts 6 and 9 on the hardwood block material (Illus. 20).

3. Use a band saw or jigsaw to cut all these parts to shape (Illus. 21).

4. Drill the axle holes into the chassis (Part 1) (Illus. 19). The diameter of these holes will depend upon the diameter of the axle required for the wheels you purchased for this project.

5. The headlights (Part 4) are made from ⅜" diameter hardwood dowel (Illus. 20). The dowel is sanded to a cone shape at its end, then cut straight off, which creates the headlight shape.

6. Sand all parts to prepare them for final assembly (Illus. 21). Radius the seats and detail as desired to promote a realistic look.

Illus. 20   Layout of parts.
1903 Fiat.

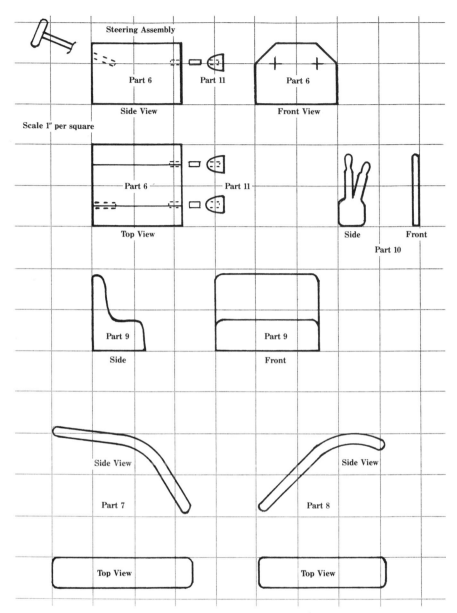

ASSEMBLY

7. Slip the rear floor (Part 2) into place on the car chassis (Part 1), and secure with carpenter's glue.

8. Refer to Illus. 22 and 23 for alignment details, and secure Parts 3, 4, 5, 6, 7, 8, and 9 into position with wood glue.

9. Drill the ⅛″ diameter mounting holes for the steering wheel shaft and the headlights (Illus. 20). Also, drill a shallow ⅛″ diameter hole into the backside of each headlight.

10. Use a short piece of ⅛″ dowel and car-penter's glue to secure each headlight into place (Illus. 20 and 24).

11. Glue the steering wheel shaft into place, and secure the steering wheel, a ¾″ diameter hardwood toy wheel, to the end with wood glue (Illus. 20 and 24).

12. Glue the gearshift and hand brake assembly (Part 10) into place on the right side of the car body (Illus. 23 and 24).

13. Paint the finished project either with non-toxic paints or varnish, to suit your tastes.

14. Add the 2″ diameter wheels and your project is ready for display.

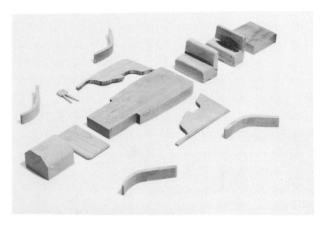

Illus. 21   Use a band saw to cut the parts to shape.

Illus. 22   Body assembled.

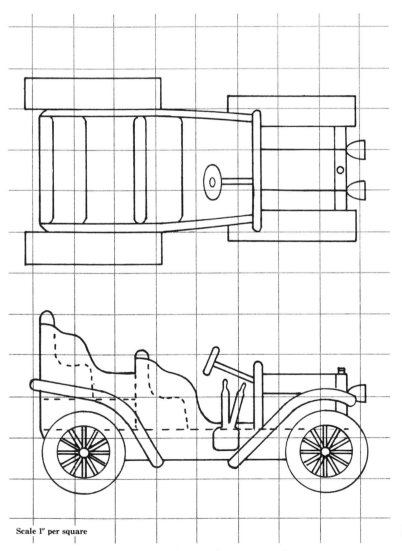

Scale 1″ per square

Illus. 23   Fiat assembled shows placement of parts.

Illus. 24

1907 Chadwick

Illus. 25

Materials List

Hardwood Stock, ¾" .... *3" × 17"*
Hardwood Block Material .... *2" × 3" × 12"*
Hardwood Dowel, ⅛" .... *6"*
Hardwood Dowel, ¼" .... *8"*
Hardwood Dowel, ⅜" .... *2"*
Hardwood Toy Wheel, ¾" .... *1 each*
Hardwood Toy Wheel, Spoked,
   2" diameter .... *4 each*
Carpenter's Glue .... *Small container*
Non-toxic varnish or paint of several colors in
   small containers

Cutting List

Part 1 ... *Car Chassis* .... *Make 1*
Part 2 ... *Engine Hood* .... *Make 1*
Part 3 ... *Fire Wall* .... *Make 1*
Part 4 ... *Forward Body* .... *Make 1*
Part 5 ... *Rear Body* .... *Make 1*
Part 6 ... *Seat* .... *Make 2*
Part 7 ... *Headlight* .... *Make 2*
Part 8 ... *Fender Assembly* ...... *Make 2*
Part 9 ... *Fender Side* .... *Make 2*
Part 10 .. *Tool Box* .... *Make 1*

Instructions

LAYOUT

1. Lay out Parts 1, 8, 9, and 10 on ¾" hardwood material (Illus. 26 and 27).

2. Lay out Parts 2, 3, 4, 5, and 6 on the hardwood block material (Illus. 26).

3. Use your band saw or jigsaw to cut each of these parts to shape (Illus. 28).

4. Drill the axle holes into the chassis (Part 1). The actual diameter of these holes will depend upon the diameter of the axle required for the wheels that you have chosen to use (Illus. 26).

5. The headlights (Part 7) are made from short pieces of ⅜" dowel.

6. Sand all finished parts to prepare them for assembly (Illus. 28). Radius the edges of seats and body parts and detail as desired to add authenticity.

ASSEMBLY

7. Drill the two ⅛" holes into the top of the chassis (Part 1), as shown in Illus. 26. These holes are the mounting holes for the gearshift and hand brake.

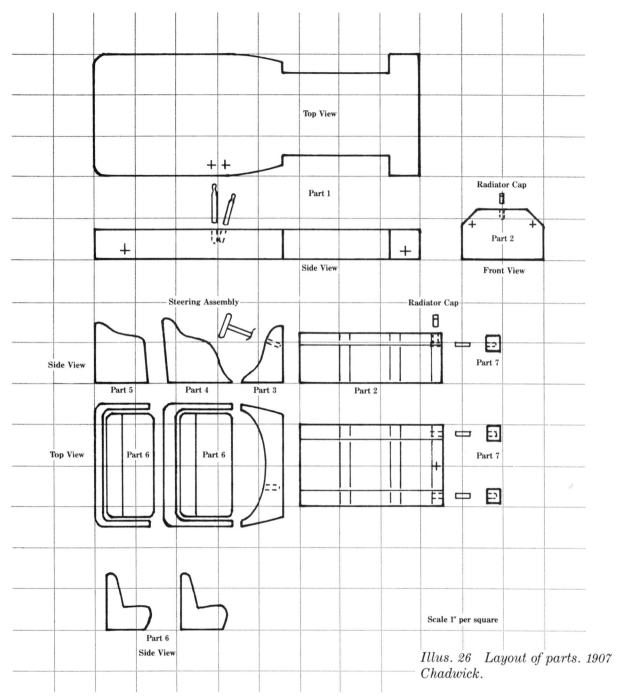

Illus. 26 Layout of parts. 1907 Chadwick.

8. The gearshift and hand brake handles are made from ⅛″ hardwood dowel. Shape the handles near the tops with small wood rasps and sandpaper.

9. After these two parts are shaped, glue them into position with wood glue.

10. Use wood glue to secure Parts 2, 3, 4, 5, and 6 into position (Illus. 29 and 30).

11. Drill ⅛″ holes, as shown in Illus. 26, for mounting the radiator cap, headlights, and steering wheel post.

12. Drill ⅛″ holes into the backsides of the headlights and use a short piece of ⅛″ dowel to align into position. Secure in place with carpenter's glue.

13. The radiator cap is simply a short piece of

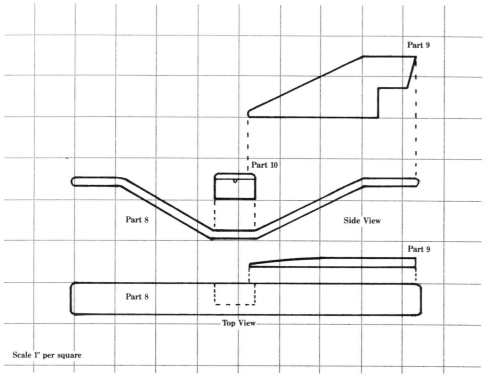

Illus. 27   Parts. 1907 Chadwick.

Part 9

Part 10

Part 8

Side View

Part 9

Part 8

Top View

Scale 1″ per square

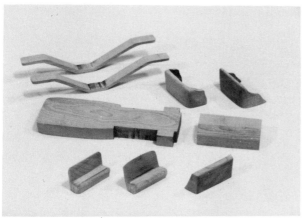

Illus. 28   Cut the parts to shape with jigsaw.

⅛″ dowel. Use a sharp knife to cut a ring near the top, to give the appearance of the cap. Glue this part into place so that it protrudes above the top of the engine hood (Part 2) by about ⅛″ (Illus. 26).

14. Cut the steering wheel post from a section of ⅛″ dowel. Secure the ¾″ hardwood toy wheel to one end with wood glue, and glue the other end into the hole drilled into the fire wall (Part 3).

15. Glue the fender sides (Part 9) to the insides of the fenders (Part 8) (Illus. 27 and 31).

16. Refer to Illus. 29 for alignment details, and glue the fender assemblies into place.

17. The tool box (Part 10) can now be glued into place on the right fender section (Illus. 27).

18. Paint or varnish the completed project at this time. Considerable detail can be achieved through careful painting.

19. Secure the 2″ spoked hardwood wheels into place, and your 1907 Chadwick is ready for display.

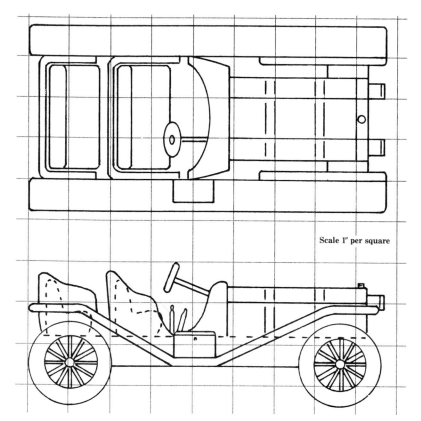

Illus. 29   Assembly details for 1907 Chadwick.

Scale 1″ per square

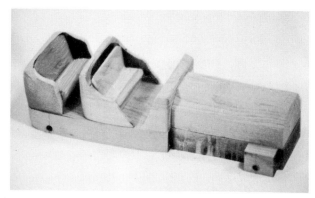

Illus. 30   Chadwick body.

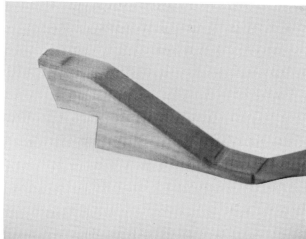

Illus. 31   Glue fender sides to insides of fenders.

Illus. 32

1910 Cadillac

Illus. 33

Materials List

Hardwood Stock, ¾" .... 3" × 20"
Hardwood Block .... 2" × 3" × 16"
Hardwood Dowel, ⅛" .... 36"
Hardwood Dowel, ¼" .... 10"
Hardwood Dowel, ⅜" .... 2"
Hardwood Toy Wheel, ¾" diameter ... 1 each
Hardwood Toy Wheels, Spoked,
  2" diameter .... 5 each
Carpenter's Glue .... Small container
Non-toxic varnish or paints, two or three col-
  ors in small containers

Cutting List

Part 1 ... Car Chassis .... Make 1
Part 2 ... Car Body .... Make 1
Part 3 ... Car Top .... Make 1
Part 4 ... Fender .... Make 2
Part 5 ... Front Seat .... Make 1
Part 6 ... Rear Seat Bottom ...... Make 1
Part 7 ... Rear Seat Back .... Make 1
Part 8 ... Headlight .... Make 2

Instructions

LAYOUT

1. Lay out Parts 1, 4, 6, and 7 on the ¾" hardwood stock (Illus. 34 and 35).

2. Lay out Parts 2, 3, and 5 on the hardwood block material (Illus. 34 and 35).

3. Use your band saw or jigsaw to cut each of these parts to shape.

4. Drill the axle holes into the chassis (Part 1) (Illus. 34). The actual size of these holes will depend upon the diameter of the axle required for the wheels you've chosen. Also, drill a hole of the same size for mounting the spare tire at the rear of the body (Part 2).

5. The headlights (Part 8) can be shaped from ⅜" dowel stock, and the side lanterns (Part 9) from ¼" dowel stock.

6. All of these parts should be shaped, radiused, detailed, and sanded at this time in preparation for assembly (Illus. 36).

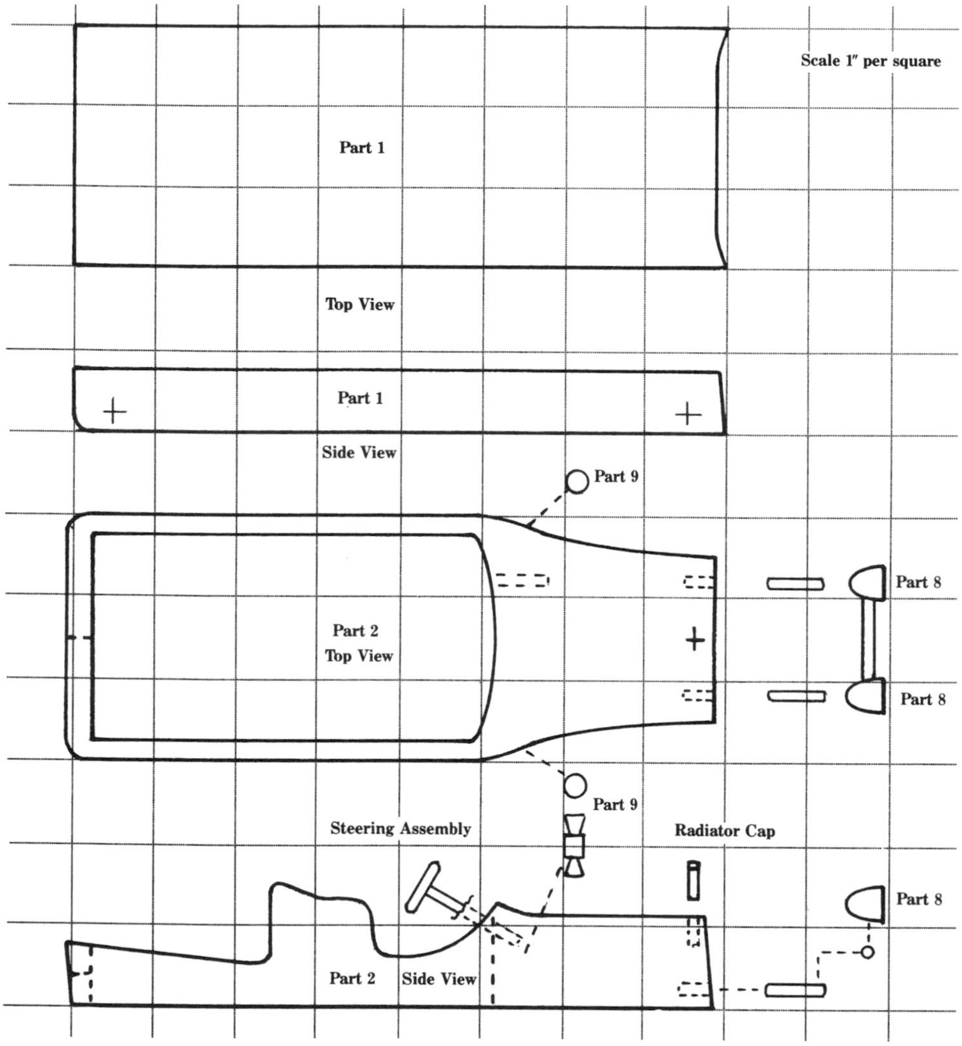

Illus. 34 Layout of parts. 1910 Cadillac.

Scale 1″ per square

Part 1

Top View

Part 1

Side View

Part 9

Part 2
Top View

Part 8

Part 8

Steering Assembly

Part 9

Radiator Cap

Part 8

Part 2 Side View

ASSEMBLY

7. Align and secure the car body (Part 2) to the chassis (Part 1), using carpenter's glue (Illus. 38).

8. Drill ⅛″ mounting holes for the steering wheel post, headlamps, and radiator cap (Illus. 34).

9. Cut the steering shaft to length from a section of ⅛″ dowel stock.

10. Glue the ¾″ diameter hardwood wheel to one end of the steering shaft, and insert the other end into the mounting hole with a drop of glue.

11. The radiator cap is a short piece of ⅛″ dowel with a radial cut or mark around one end. This mark can be made with a sharp knife (Illus. 34).

12. Glue the radiator cap into place so that it extends above the engine hood by about ⅛″ (Illus. 34).

13. Glue two ⅛″ dowel sections into the headlight mounting holes, so that they extend ½″ beyond the front of the body (Part 2) (Illus. 34).

14. Glue a 1½″ section of ⅛″ dowel across the headlight mounting brackets at the extended end (Illus. 34).

15. Now glue the headlights (Part 8) into place at the ends of the cross bracket. To add strength, file a small groove into the bottom-side of each headlamp with a small round file or wood rasp. This creates a saddle, to allow the parts to fit together more readily (Illus. 34).

16. Glue the side lantern (Part 9) into place at each side of the body (Part 2).

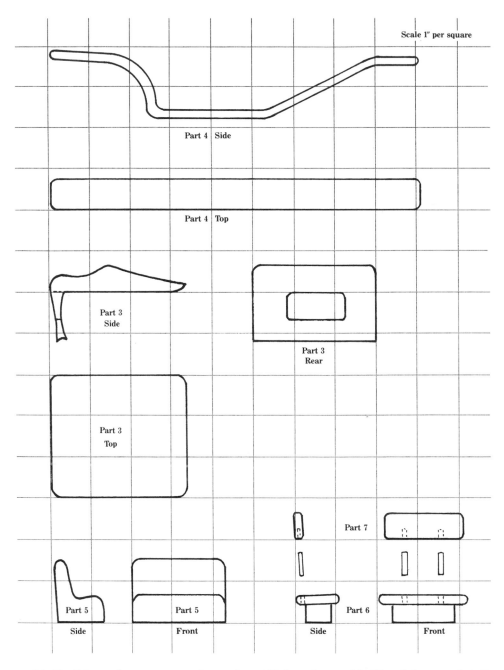

Illus. 35   Parts. 1910 Cadillac.

17. Build up the rear seat by using ⅛″ dowel sections; use them to support the seat back (Part 7), as shown in Illus. 35 and 37.

18. Glue the front seat and the rear seat assembly into place (Illus. 38).

19. Align and glue the fenders (Part 4) to each side of the vehicle (Illus. 38).

20. Using ⅛″ dowel sections, as shown in Illus. 38 and 39, glue the top (Part 3) into place.

21. Varnish or paint the finished body assembly as you desire. Again, careful painting can add a great deal of authenticity to your completed project.

22. Secure the five 2″ spoked hardwood toy wheels into place at this time.

23. Your 1910 Cadillac is now complete and ready for use or display as you choose.

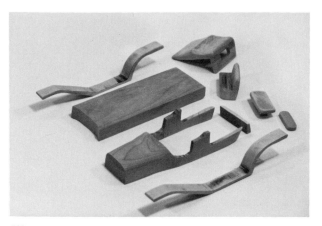

Illus. 36   Cut parts to shape.

Illus. 37   Use ⅛″ dowel sections to support seat back.

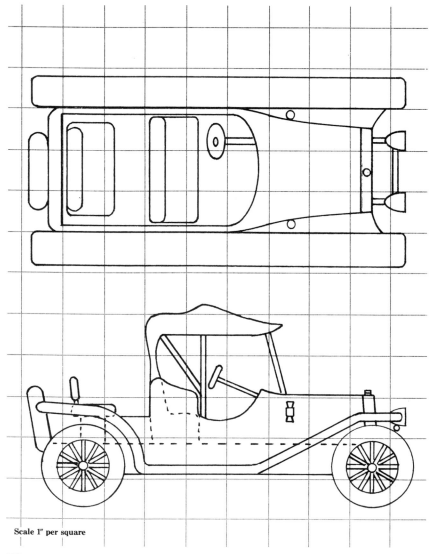

Scale 1″ per square

Illus. 38   Assembly details for 1910 Cadillac.

Illus. 39

· 3 ·
COMING UP IN THE WORLD

By the mid 1920s, the automobile had pretty much won the battle with the horsedrawn carriage; it had become a respected means of transportation, and not just a fad or a fun thing to do. By this time it had also undergone some fairly substantial evolutionary changes. With a quarter of a century of experience, the carmakers were now able to produce cars that were (somewhat) mechanically sound and held at least a promise of reliability. Furthermore, designs and styles were beginning to come into play. There was, on the one hand, a car with enclosed compartments and conservative designs, which provided a gentleman and his family with warm, comfortable transportation. On the other hand, there was a car with a sporty style, with convertible tops, rumbling engines, and an all-around more flashy look. It was during this period that the automobile became a means by which many persons expressed themselves and established their identities.

It is the idea of self-expression within the design of these cars that is responsible for their standing as true "classics." Display one of these babies on your coffee table and see if you don't start some conversation!

1925 Model "T" Ford

Illus. 40

Materials List

Hardwood Stock, ¾" .... *3" × 22"*
Hardwood Block .... *2" × 3" × 25"*
Hardwood Dowel, ⅛" diameter .... *6"*
Hardwood Dowel, ¼" diameter .... *10"*
Hardwood Dowel, ⅜" diameter .... *2"*
Hardwood Toy Wheel, ¾" diameter ... *1 each*
Hardwood Toy Wheels, Spoked,
    2" diameter .... *4 each*
Carpenter's Glue .... *Small container*
Non-toxic varnish or two or three colors of
    paint in small containers

Cutting List

Part 1	... *Chassis*	*Make 1*
Part 2	... *Engine Hood*	*Make 1*
Part 3	... *Rear Body*	*Make 1*
Part 4	... *Right Door*	*Make 1*
Part 5	... *Left Door*	*Make 1*
Part 6	... *Fender*	*Make 2*
Part 7	... *Top*	*Make 1*
Part 8	... *Seat*	*Make 1*
Part 9	... *Front Bumper*	*Make 1*
Part 10	.. *Rear Bumper*	*Make 1*
Part 11	.. *Headlight*	*Make 2*

Instructions

LAYOUT

1. Lay out the chassis (Part 1), the doors (Parts 4 and 5), two fenders (Part 6), and the front and rear bumpers (Parts 9 and 10) on ¾" hardwood stock (Illus. 41 and 42).

2. On the hardwood block material, lay out the engine hood (Part 2), the rear body (Part 3), the top (Part 7), and the seat (Part 8) (Illus. 41 and 42).

3. Cut all of these parts to shape using a band saw or jigsaw (Illus. 43).

4. Shape the headlights (Part 11) from ⅜" diameter dowel (Illus. 41).

5. Shape, radius, detail, and sand these parts to prepare them for assembly (Illus. 43 and 44).

ASSEMBLY

6. Drill the axle holes (Illus. 41) through the chassis (Part 1). The size of these holes will be determined by the axle size and wheel size.

7. Drill the two 9/64" door hinge holes into the top of the chassis (Part 1), and into the bottom of each door (Parts 4 and 5) (Illus. 41).

8. Glue a short ⅛" dowel section into the hole at the bottom of each door. Place these door pins into the holes in the chassis (Part 1), but DO NOT GLUE (Illus. 45).

9. Use wood glue to secure the engine hood (Part 2) and the rear body (Part 3) to the chassis (Part 1). Illus. 46 shows the proper alignment of these parts; however, the prior placement of the doors (Parts 4 and 5) should be taken into consideration.

> **NOTE:** The front edges of the doors (Parts 4 and 5) can be rounded slightly to allow easier operation.

10. Align and glue the fenders (Part 6) into place (Illus. 46).

11. Drill the ⅛" holes for mounting the steering shaft, windshield post, headlights, radiator cap, and taillight (Illus. 41 and 42).

12. The taillight is a piece of ⅛" dowel with a rounded end, which furthers the appearance of a taillight. Glue this part into place (Illus. 42).

13. Glue the ¾" hardwood toy wheel to one end of a ⅛" dowel, and insert the other end into the steering shaft mounting hole with a drop of glue (Illus. 41).

14. Cut two ⅛" dowel sections for the windshield post, and glue in place so that they each extend above the engine hood (Part 2) by 1¼" (Illus. 41).

15. Drill a ⅛" mounting hole into the backside of each headlight (Part 11). Use a short piece of ⅛" dowel and wood glue to fasten each headlight into place (Illus. 41).

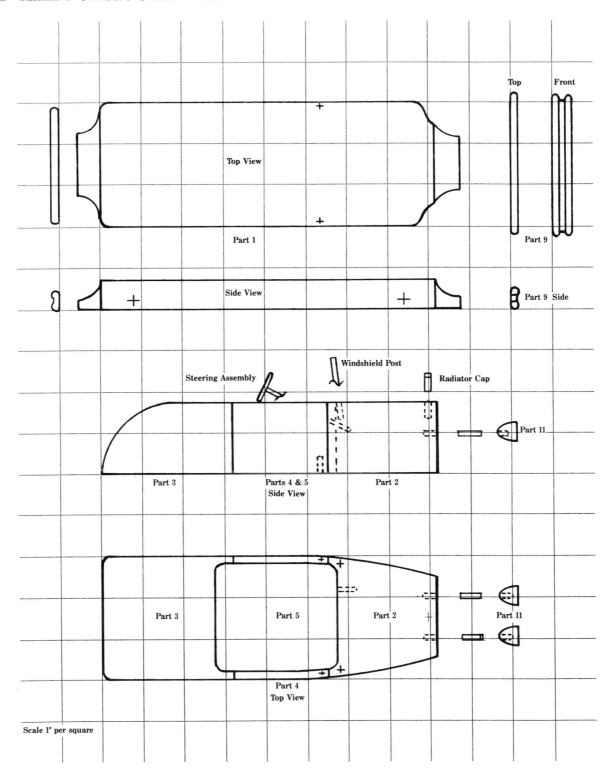

Top

Front

Top View

Part 1

Part 9

Side View

Part 9 Side

Steering Assembly

Windshield Post

Radiator Cap

Part 11

Part 3

Parts 4 & 5
Side View

Part 2

Part 3

Part 5

Part 2

Part 11

Part 4
Top View

Scale 1″ per square

Illus. 41   Layout of parts. Model "T" Ford.

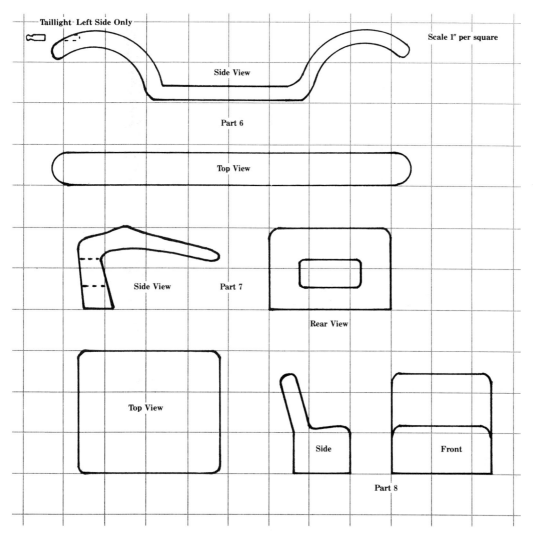

Taillight Left Side Only

Scale 1″ per square

Side View

Part 6

Top View

Side View   Part 7

Rear View

Top View

Side   Front

Part 8

Illus. 42 More parts. Model "T" Ford.

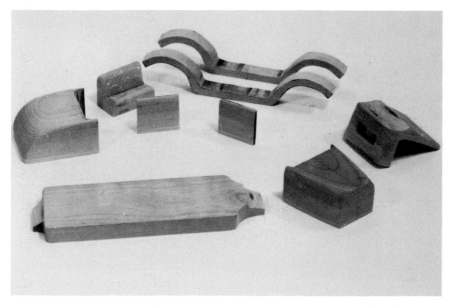

Illus. 43 Use a band saw to cut these parts to shape.

16. The radiator cap is a short piece of ⅛″ dowel. It may be detailed with a shallow ring cut near the end, for the sake of authenticity.

17. Glue the seat (Part 8) into place.

18. Align and glue the top (Part 7) into place (Illus. 46 and 47).

19. Align and glue the front and rear bumpers (Parts 9 and 10) into place (Illus. 41, 47, and 48).

20. Varnish or paint the complete assembly at this time. Again, much detail can be achieved through careful painting.

21. Mount the four 2″ spoked hardwood wheels.

22. This project is now complete and ready for play or display.

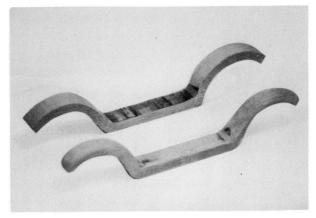

Illus. 44 Shape, radius, and detail all parts.

Illus. 45 Place the door pins into the holes in the chassis, but do not glue.

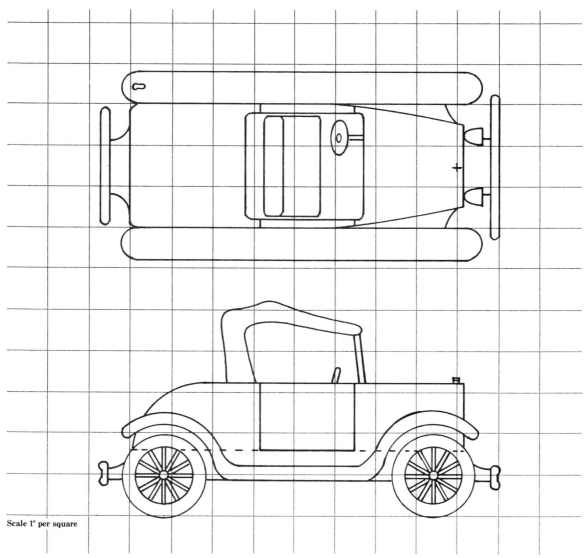

Scale 1" per square

Illus. 46   Assembly details for 1925 Model "T" Ford.

Illus. 47   1925 Model "T" assembled.

Illus. 48   Another view, Model "T" assembled.

Stutz Bearcat

Illus. 49

Materials List

Hardwood Stock, ¾" .... 5" × 22"
Hardwood Block .... 2" × 3" × 10"
Hardwood Dowel, ⅛" diameter .... 12"
Hardwood Dowel, ¼" diameter .... 8"
Hardwood Dowel, ⅜" diameter .... 2"
Hardwood Dowel, 1" diameter .... 3"
Hardwood Toy Wheel, ¾" diameter ... 1 each
Hardwood Toy Wheels, Spoked,
  2" diameter .... 6 each
Carpenter's Glue .... Small container
Non-toxic varnish or two or three colors of
  paint in small containers

Cutting List

Part 1 ... Chassis .... Make 1
Part 2 ... Engine Hood .... Make 1
Part 3 ... Seat/Body .... Make 1
Part 4 ... Seat .... Make 2
Part 5 ... Tank Support .... Make 1
Part 6 ... Gas Tank .... Make 1
Part 7 ... Luggage Compartment . Make 1
Part 8 ... Fender .... Make 2
Part 9 ... Fender Side .... Make 2
Part 10 .. Rear Bumper .... Make 1
Part 11 .. Headlight .... Make 2

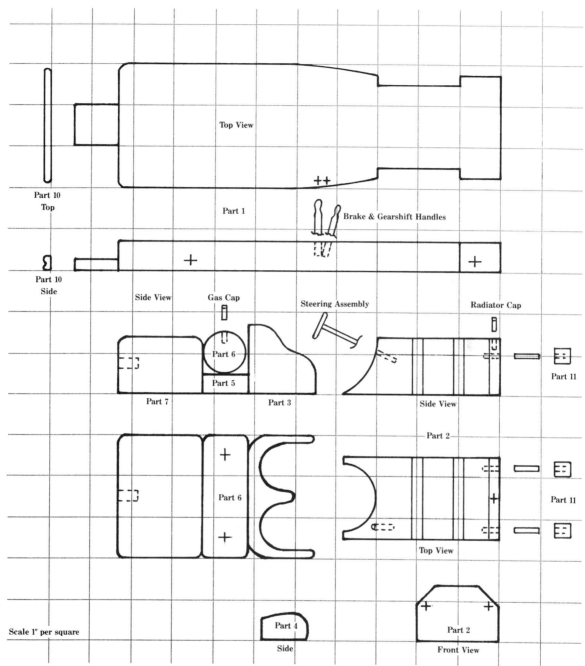

Illus. 50   Layout of parts. Stutz Bearcat.

Instructions

LAYOUT

1. Lay out the chassis (Part 1), two seats (Part 3), the tank support (Part 5), two fenders and fender sides (Parts 8 and 9), and the rear bumper (Part 10) on ¾″ hardwood stock (Illus. 50, 51, and 52).

2. Using the hardwood block material, lay out the engine hood (Part 2), the seat/body (Part 3), and the luggage compartment (Part 7) (Illus. 50 and 52).

3. Using your band saw or jigsaw, cut all of the parts to shape (Illus. 52).

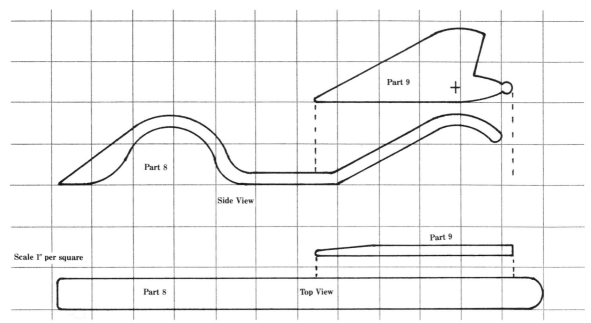

Illus. 51   Parts. Stutz Bearcat.

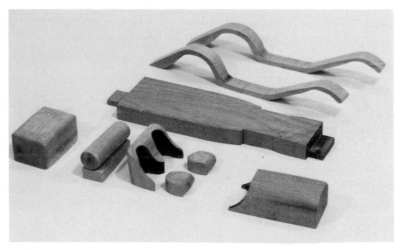

Illus. 52   Prepare all parts for assembly.

4. The headlights (Part 11) are made from ⅜″ diameter dowel (Illus. 50).

5. The gas tank (Part 6) is made from a 1″ diameter dowel (Illus. 50).

6. Shape, radius, detail, and sand all parts to prepare them for assembly (Illus. 52).

ASSEMBLY

7. Drill the axle holes (Illus. 50) through the chassis (Part 1). The size of the holes will depend upon the wheels that you've chosen and the required axle size for those wheels.

8. Drill the hole for mounting the spare tires into the rear side of the luggage compartment (Part 7). This hole will be the same size as the axle holes.

9. Using carpenter's glue, align and secure the engine hood (Part 2), the seat/body (Part 3), the tank support (Part 5), the luggage compartment (Part 7), the gas tank (Part 6), and the two seats (Part 4) in place (Illus. 54 and 55).

Illus. 53   Glue a fender side to the inside of each fender.

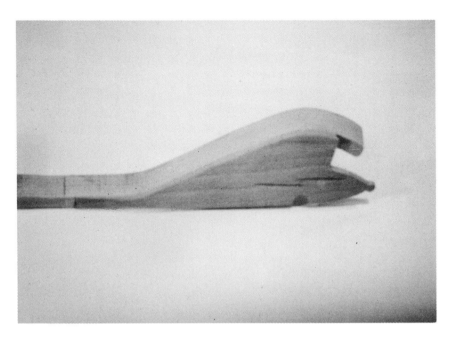

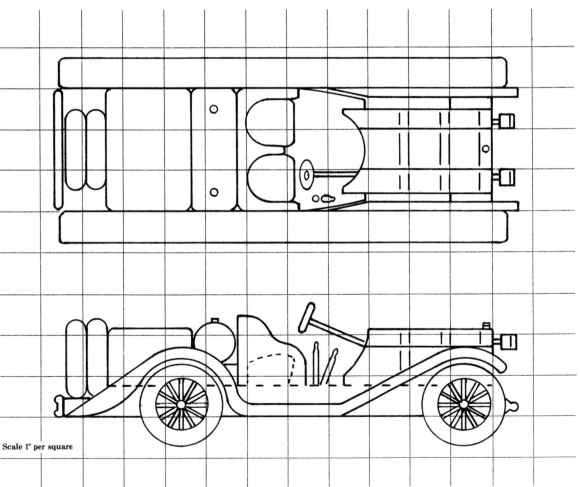

Scale 1″ per square

Illus. 54   Assembly details for Stutz Bearcat.

10. Glue the fender sides (Part 9) to the fenders (Part 8). The fender sides are to be located on the insides of the fenders, next to the engine hood when mounted (Illus. 51 and 53).

11. Align and glue the fender assemblies into place (Illus. 54).

12. Drill ⅛″ holes for mounting the steering shaft, gearshift and brake lever, headlights, radiator cap, and gas tank caps (Illus. 50 and 54).

13. Glue the ¾″ diameter hardwood toy wheel to one end of a 2″ (5.08 cm) section of ⅛″ diameter hardwood dowel. Insert the other end of this dowel section into the steering shaft mounting hole, using a drop of wood glue to secure it in place (Illus. 50).

14. The gearshift and brake levers are also ⅛″ dowel sections. Each one is approximately 1½″ in length, and has one end shaped with sandpaper, so as to resemble a handle grip (Illus. 50). These should be made and installed at this time.

15. Install the headlights, as shown in Illus. 50 and 54, using carpenter's glue and ⅛″ dowel sections approximately ½″ long. Insert the dowel sections into ⅛″ diameter mounting holes in the front of the engine hood and in the rear of each headlight.

16. The radiator cap and gas tank caps are short sections of ⅛″ dowel. Glue into the holes provided. They should extend above the surface approximately ⅛″, and may have shallow rings cut in them, to give them the appearance of caps. (Illus. 50 and 54).

17. Align and glue the rear bumper (Part 10) into place (Illus. 50 and 54).

18. The finished assembly may be painted or varnished at this time.

19. Mount the six 2″ spoked hardwood wheels. Two wheels are to be mounted as spare tires. The length and diameter of the hardwood dowel axles will depend upon the actual wheels that you use.

20. Your Stutz Bearcat is now complete and may be proudly displayed.

Illus. 55

1936 Triumph Roadster

Illus. 56

Materials List

Hardwood Stock, ¾"	....	*5" × 24"*
Hardwood Block	....	*2" × 3" × 15"*
Hardwood Dowel, ⅛" diameter	....	*15"*
Hardwood Dowel, ¼" diameter	....	*8"*
Hardwood Dowel, ⅜" diameter	....	*2"*
Hardwood Toy Wheel, ¾" diameter	...	*1 each*
Hardwood Toy Wheel, 2" diameter	...	*5 each*
Carpenter's Glue	....	*Small container*
Non-toxic varnish or two or three colors of paint in small containers		

Cutting List

Part 1	...	*Chassis*	*Make 1*
Part 2	...	*Engine Hood*	*Make 1*
Part 3	...	*Rear Body*	*Make 1*
Part 4	...	*Right Door*	*Make 1*
Part 5	...	*Left Door*	*Make 1*
Part 6	...	*Right Fender*	*Make 1*
Part 7	...	*Left Fender*	*Make 1*
Part 8	...	*Convertible Top*	*Make 1*
Part 9	...	*Bumper*	*Make 2*
Part 10	..	*Headlamp*	*Make 2*
Part 11	..	*Seat*	*Make 1*

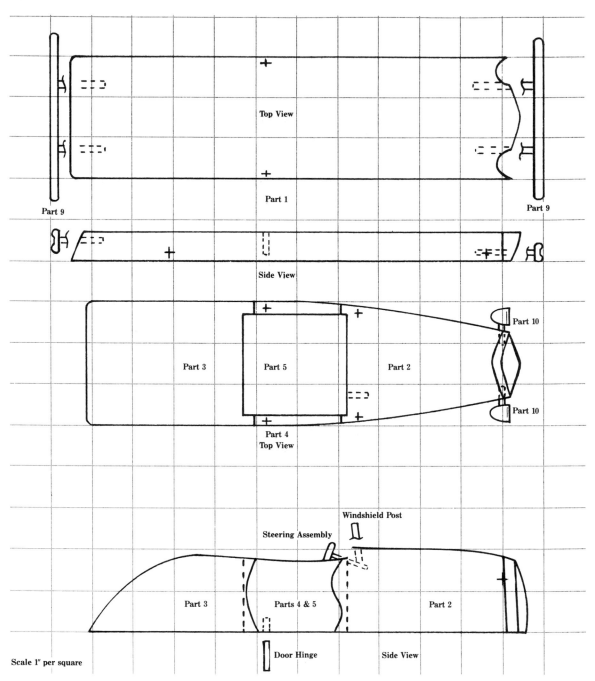

Illus. 57   Layout of parts. 1936 Triumph.

Instructions

LAYOUT

1. Lay out the chassis (Part 1), the right and left doors (Parts 4 and 5), the right and left fenders (Parts 6 and 7), and the bumpers (Part 9) on the ¾″ hardwood stock (Illus. 57 and 58).

2. Lay out the engine hood (Part 2), the rear body (Part 3), the convertible top (Part 8), and the seat (Part 11) on the hardwood block material (Illus. 57 and 58).

3. Cut all of these parts to shape using your band saw or jigsaw (Illus. 57, 58, and 59).

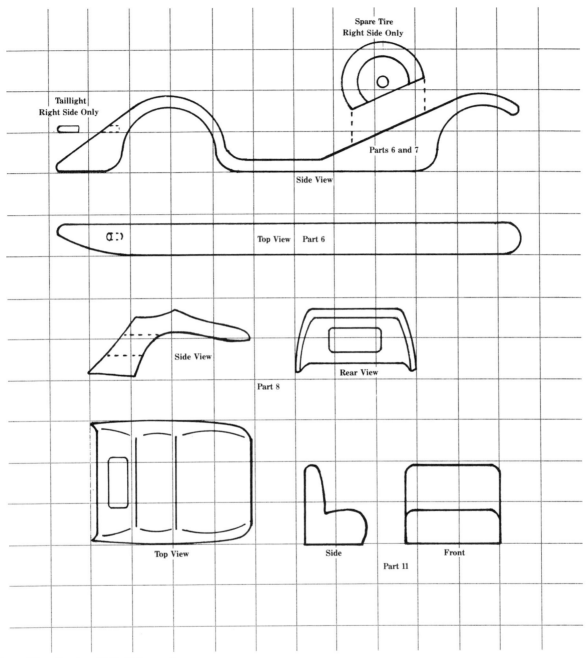

Spare Tire
Right Side Only

Taillight
Right Side Only

Side View

Parts 6 and 7

Top View   Part 6

Side View

Rear View

Part 8

Top View

Side

Front

Part 11

Illus. 58   Parts. 1936 Triumph.

4. The headlights (Part 10) are shaped from sections of ⅜″ dowel (Illus. 57).

5. Make the spare tire by cutting off a section from a 2″ diameter toy wheel, thereby creating a flat side for mounting (Illus. 58).

6. Shape, radius, detail, and sand all of these parts to prepare them for assembly (Illus. 57, 58, and 59).

NOTE: The right and left doors (Parts 4 and 5) have the same appearance when viewed from the side, but not when viewed from above; there is a right-side door and a left-side door. The same is true for the right and left fenders (Parts 6 and 7).

Illus. 59   Cut all of these parts to shape with your band saw or jigsaw.

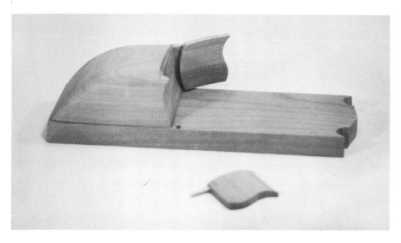

Illus. 60   Place the doors into position on the chassis. Do not glue.

ASSEMBLY

7. Drill the axle holes through the chassis (Part 1). The size of these holes will depend upon the size of the axle. If you use a ¼" axle, then drill ⁹⁄₃₂" diameter holes, to allow room for the axles to turn (Illus. 57).

8. Drill the ⅛" holes for mounting the headlights, the windshield post, the steering shaft, and the front and rear bumpers (Illus. 57).

9. Drill ⁹⁄₆₄" holes into the chassis (Part 1), for the door hinges (Illus. 57).

10. Drill ⅛" holes into the bottom sides of the doors (Parts 4 and 5), for the hinge pins to mount into (Illus. 57).

11. Make the door hinge pins from sections of ⅛" dowel, each approximately ¾" in length.

12. Glue these dowel sections into the holes in the bottom sides of the doors. Place the doors into position on the chassis (Part 1). Do not glue (Illus. 57, 60, and 61).

13. Glue the engine hood (Part 2) and the rear body (Part 3) into place on the chassis (Part 1) (Illus. 60 and 61). Allow enough room for the doors to pivot smoothly to the open and closed positions. You may need to round the edges of the doors slightly to improve their pivot operations.

14. Align the fenders (Parts 6 and 7) into position and secure with carpenter's glue (Illus. 61 and 62).

15. Attach the spare tire to the right fender with glue (Illus. 58, 61, and 62).

16. Mount the headlights (Part 10), the front and rear bumpers (Part 9), and the windshield post, as shown in Illus. 57, 61, and 62.

17. Place the seat (Part 11) into position and secure with carpenter's glue (Illus. 61).

18. The steering shaft is a 2" length of ⅛" diameter dowel.

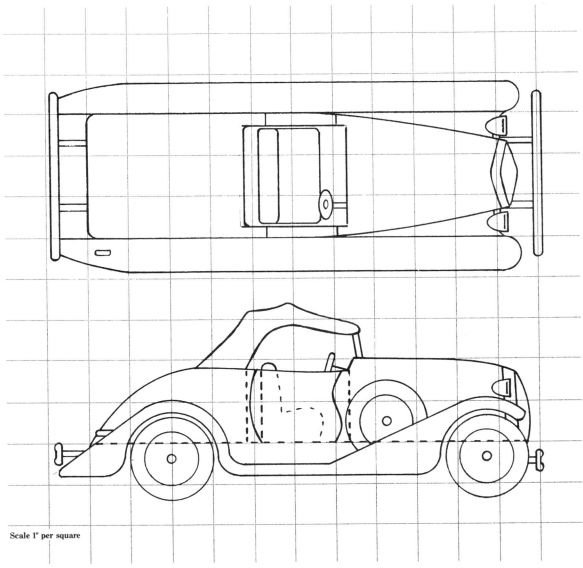

Scale 1″ per square

Illus. 61   Assembly and parts location details for 1936 Triumph Roadster.

19. Glue the ¾″ diameter hardwood toy wheel to one end of the steering shaft, and glue the other end of the shaft into the hole at the rear of the engine hood (Illus. 57).

20. This would be a good time to varnish or paint the partially completed project.

21. Secure the convertible top in place with wood glue (Illus. 61 and 62).

22. Install the four 2″ hardwood toy wheels using the appropriate hardwood dowels as axles (Illus. 62).

23. The Triumph Roadster is now complete and ready for use.

Illus. 62

Duesenberg SSJ

Illus. 63

Materials List

Hardwood Stock, ¾"	*5" × 24"*
Hardwood Block	*2" × 3" × 15"*
Hardwood Dowel, ⅛" diameter	*18"*
Hardwood Dowel, ⅜" diameter	*2"*
Hardwood Toy Wheel, ¾" diameter ...	*1 each*
Hardwood Toy Wheels, 2" diameter ..	*5 each*
Carpenter's Glue	*Small container*
Non-toxic varnish or two or three colors of	
paint in small containers	

Cutting List

Part 1	...	*Chassis*	....	*Make 1*
Part 2	...	*Engine Hood*	....	*Make 1*
Part 3	...	*Rear Body*	....	*Make 1*
Part 4	...	*Door*	....	*Make 2*
Part 5	...	*Seat*	....	*Make 1*
Part 6	...	*Fender*	....	*Make 2*
Part 7	...	*Fender Side*	....	*Make 2*
Part 8	...	*Convertible Top Boot*	...	*Make 1*
Part 9	...	*Front Bumper*	....	*Make 1*
Part 10	..	*Rear Bumper*	....	*Make 1*
Part 11	..	*Headlight*	....	*Make 2*

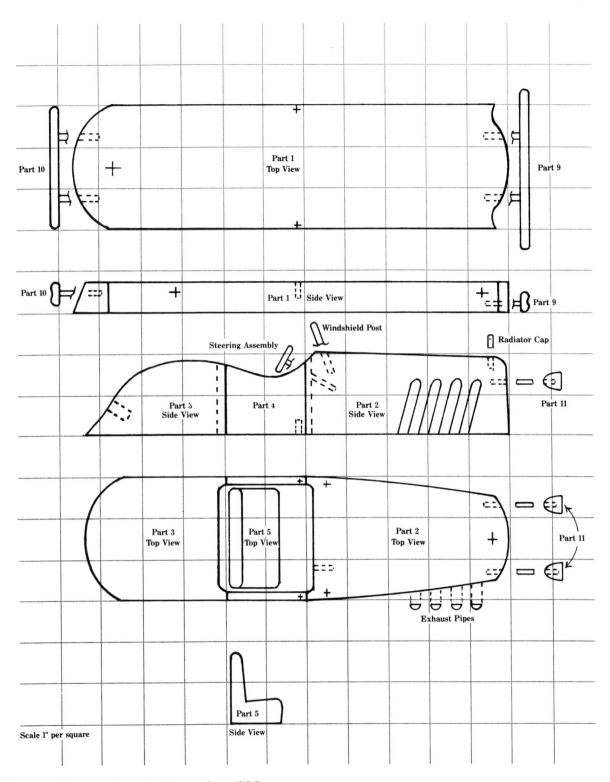

Illus. 64   Layout of parts. Duesenberg SSJ.

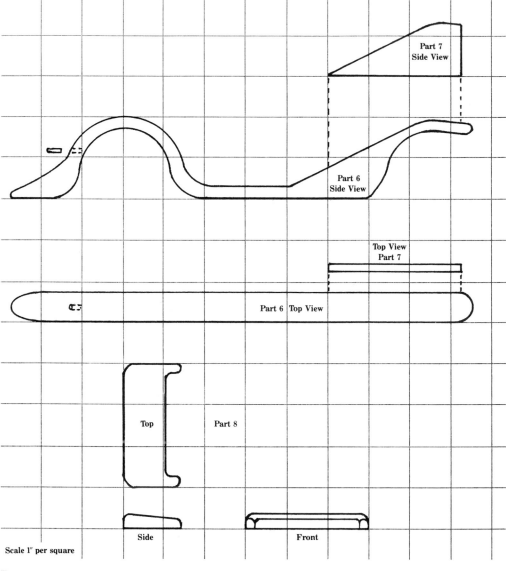

Illus. 65 Parts. Duesenberg SSJ.

Part 7
Side View

Part 6
Side View

Top View
Part 7

Part 6 Top View

Top   Part 8

Side   Front

Scale 1″ per square

Instructions

LAYOUT

1. Lay out the chassis (Part 1), two doors (Part 4), two fender (Part 6), two fenders sides (Part 7), the convertible top boot (Part 8), and the front and rear bumpers (Parts 9 and 10) on the ¾″ hardwood stock (Illus. 64 and 65).

2. Layout the engine hood (Part 2), the rear body (Part 3), and the seat (Part 5) on the hardwood block material (Illus. 64).

3. Use your band saw or jigsaw to cut these parts to shape (Illus. 66).

4. The headlights are to be shaped from ⅜″ diameter hardwood dowel sections (Illus. 64).

5. The exhaust pipes located on the right side of the engine hood (Part 2) are made from ¼″ diameter dowel sections, each having one side sanded flat (Illus. 64).

6. Shape, radius, detail, and sand all of the parts as desired, to prepare them for final assembly (Illus. 66).

ASSEMBLY

7. Drill the axle holes into the chassis (Part 1). These holes must be sized appropriately, according to the axle diameter required for the wheels that you choose to use (Illus. 64).

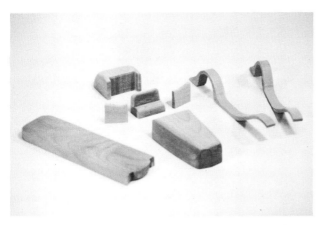

Illus. 66   Cut Duesenberg parts to shape with a band saw.

Illus. 67   Place the doors into position on the chassis. Do not glue.

8. Locate and drill all ⅛″ diameter holes required for mounting the front and rear bumpers, the headlights, the radiator cap, the windshield post, the steering column, and the taillight (Illus. 64 and 65).

9. Drill two ⁹⁄₆₄″ holes into the chassis (Part 1) for the door hinge pins to mount into (Illus. 64).

10. Drill ⅛″ diameter holes into the bottoms of the doors for the hinge pins.

11. The door hinge pins are to be cut from ⅛″ dowels.

12. Glue the hinge pins into the holes at the bottoms of the doors.

13. Place the doors on the chassis by inserting the hinge pins into the holes provided. Do not glue (Illus. 67).

14. Glue the engine hood (Part 2), the rear body (Part 3), and the seat (Part 5) into place as shown (Illus. 67 and 68).

> **NOTE:** Allow enough room between the engine hood and the rear body for the doors (Part 4), to permit them to operate properly. Proper operation of the doors may require that their edges be sanded.

15. Locate and glue the exhaust pipes to the right side of the engine hood (Illus. 64, 68, and 69).

16. Glue the fender sides (Part 7) to the insides of the fenders (Part 6) (Illus. 65).

17. Align and glue the fender assemblies into place at both sides of the body assembly (Illus. 68 and 69).

18. Drill a ¼″ hole, as indicated, to allow for the mounting of the spare tire to the rear of Part 3 (Illus. 64 and 69).

19. Mount the spare tire with a short section of ¼″ dowel, used for alignment. Glue in place.

20. Using short sections of ⅛″ dowel and carpenter's glue, attach the headlights (Part 11), the front and rear bumpers (Parts 9 and 10), the radiator cap, the windshield post, the steering column, and the taillight (Illus. 64, 65, 68, and 69).

21. The windshield can be completed by glueing a section of ⅛″ dowel across the top of the windshield posts (Illus. 69).

22. The ¾″ hardwood toy wheel should be glued to the steering shaft now (Illus. 69).

23. Glue the convertible top boot (Part 8) in place (Illus. 68).

24. Using dowel axles of the appropriate size, mount the four 2″ hardwood toy wheels (Illus. 68 and 69).

25. Enjoy displaying your new Duesenberg SSJ. By the way, only two of these cars were ever built!

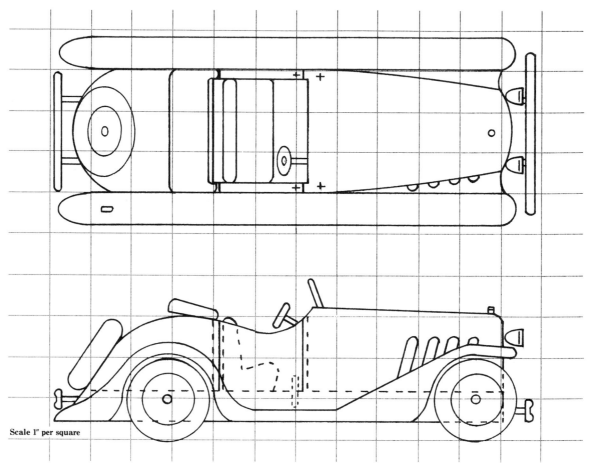

Scale 1″ per square

Illus. 68   Final assembly details. Duesenberg SSJ.

Illus. 69

· 4 ·
THE ROADSTERS

The sporty styling in automobiles really took hold. The idea became so popular that some auto manufacturers produced "sports cars" only. They were generally small vehicles with only enough room for two people and a little bit of luggage. They almost always had convertible tops and powerful engines, and were easy to handle even at higher speeds. Of course, they were stylish and sporty and held an air of distinction for their owners and drivers.

The cars in this chapter were the forerunners of our present-day sports cars. The actual cars are still sought after today and some are still in operation. They are easy and fun to build and make great gifts for those friends who have everything.

1935 Mercedes
500K Special

Illus. 70

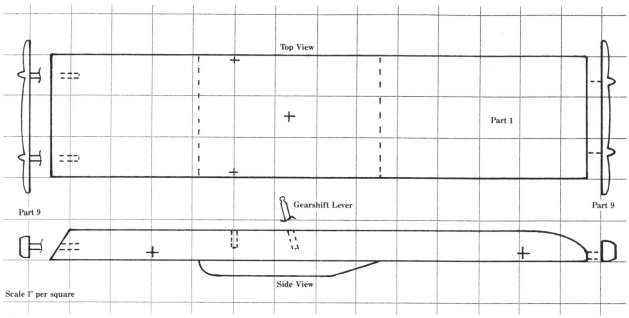

Illus. 71 Layout of parts. Mercedes 500K Special.

Materials List

Hardwood Stock, ¾″ . . . . 3″ × 36″
Hardwood Block . . . . 2″ × 3″ × 15″
Hardwood Dowel, ⅛″ diameter . . . . 15″
Hardwood Dowel, ¼″ diameter . . . . 8″
Hardwood Dowel, ⅜″ diameter . . . . 2″
Hardwood Toy Wheel, ¾″ diameter . . . 1 each
Hardwood Toy Wheels, 2″ diameter . . 6 each
Carpenter's Glue . . . . Small container
Non-toxic varnish or two or three colors of
   paint in small containers

Cutting List

Part 1 . . . Chassis . . . . Make 1
Part 2 . . . Engine Hood . . . . Make 1
Part 3 . . . Rear Body . . . . Make 1
Part 4 . . . Door . . . . Make 2
Part 5 . . . Seat . . . . Make 1
Part 6 . . . Left Fender . . . . Make 1
Part 7 . . . Right Fender . . . . Make 1
Part 8 . . . Fender Side . . . . Make 2
Part 9 . . . Front and Rear
             Bumper . . . . Make 2
Part 10 . . Headlight . . . . Make 2
Part 11 . . Center Road Lamp . . . . . Make 1
Part 12 . . Convertible Top Boot . . . Make 1

Instructions

LAYOUT

1. Lay out the chassis (Part 1), two doors (Part 4), two fenders (Parts 6 and 7), two fender sides (Part 8), two bumpers (Part 9), and the convertible top boot (Part 12) on ¾″ hardwood stock (Illus. 71, 72, and 73).

2. Lay out the engine hood (Part 2), the rear body (Part 3), and the seat (Part 5) on the hardwood block material (Illus. 72 and 73).

3. Use your band saw or jigsaw to cut all of these parts to shape (Illus. 71, 72, 73, and 74).

4. Using a section of ⅜″ diameter dowel stock, shape the two headlights, as shown in Illus. 72.

5. Shape, radius, detail, and sand these parts to prepare them for final assembly (Illus. 74 and 75).

ASSEMBLY

6. Drill the axle holes through the chassis (Part 1). The diameter of these holes will depend upon the axle size required for the wheels that you have chosen (Illus. 71).

7. Drill all ⅛″ holes for mounting the bumpers, headlight mounting bar, radiator cap,

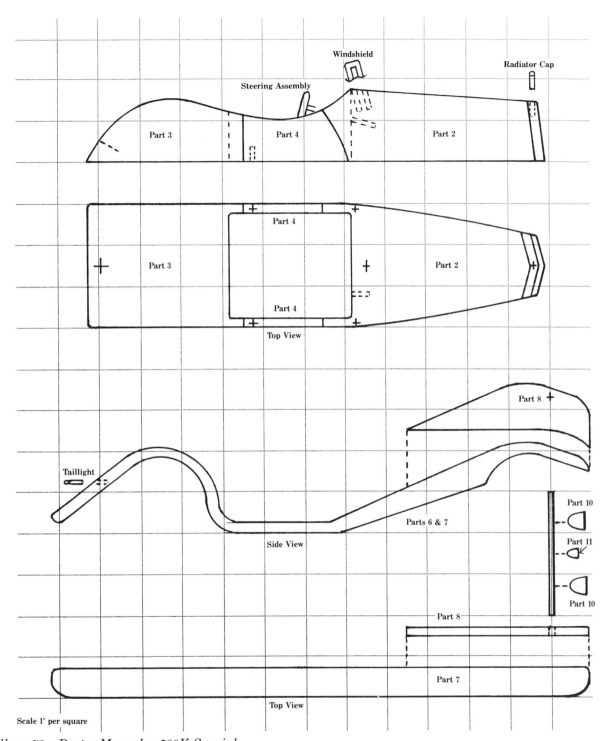

Illus. 72   Parts. Mercedes 500K Special.

gearshift, steering shaft, and windshield post (Illus. 71 and 72).

8. Drill a ¼″ hole in the rear of Part 3, as shown, for mounting the spare tires (Illus. 72).

9. Drill a ⅛″ hinge pin hole into the bottom of each of the doors (Part 4).

10. Drill a ⁹⁄₆₄″ diameter hole into the Chassis (Part 1) at each door hinge location (Illus. 71).

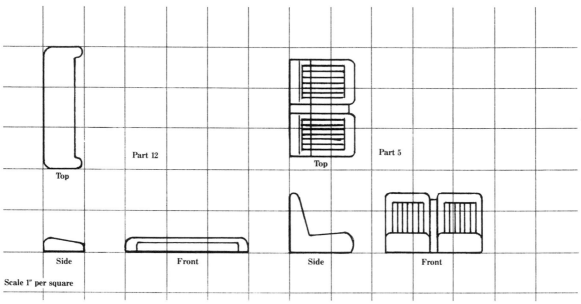

Part 12

Top

Side

Front

Part 5

Top

Side

Front

Scale 1″ per square

Illus. 73   Parts. Mercedes 500K Special.

Illus. 74   Shape, radius, detail, and sand these parts.

Illus. 75   Glue the fender sides to the insides of the fenders.

11. Make the hinge pins from short sections of ⅛″ diameter dowel. Glue these hinge pins into the holes in the bottoms of the doors.

12. Install the doors in the chassis by placing the hinge pins into the holes made for that purpose (Illus. 76).

13. Place the engine hood (Part 2) and the rear body (Part 3) on the chassis (Part 1), and align so that the doors operate properly (Illus. 77). You may find it helpful for door operation to round the hinged sides of the doors slightly.

14. Glue the fender sides (Part 8) to the insides of the fenders, as indicated in Illus. 72 and 75.

15. Align and glue the fender assemblies into place on the sides of the body of the car (Illus. 77 and 78).

16. Using short sections of ⅛″ dowel, as shown in Illus. 71, 72 and 77, mount the headlights, bumpers, radiator cap, steering shaft, and windshield post.

17. Glue the ¾″ diameter hardwood toy

Illus. 76   Install the doors by plac-
ing the hinge pins into the holes.

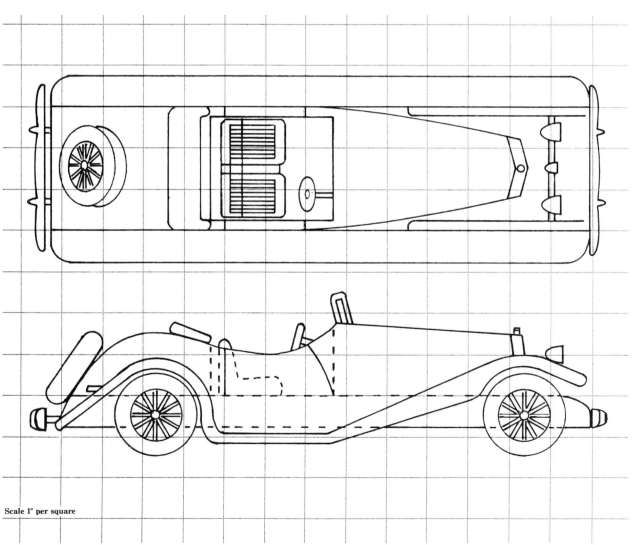

Scale 1″ per square

Illus. 77   Final assembly details for Mercedes 500K Special.

Illus. 78   Completed Mercedes 500K Special.

wheel to the top of the steering shaft to form the steering wheel.

18. Complete the windshield frame by gluing a section of ⅛″ dowel across the two windshield posts and sanding the corners to a nice smooth shape (Illus. 78).

19. Glue the seat (Part 5) and the convertible top boot (Part 12) into place (Illus. 77).

20. At this time, the project should be completely varnished or painted to suit your taste.

21. Mount the two spare tires and the running tires using the 2″ hardwood toy wheels (Illus. 77 and 78).

22. You may now enjoy displaying your finished Mercedes 500K Special.

1938 Jaguar SS-100

Illus. 79

Materials List

Hardwood Stock, ¾" .... 3" × 30"
Hardwood Block .... 2" × 3" × 15"
Hardwood Dowel, ⅛" .... 20"
Hardwood Dowel, ¼" .... 8"
Hardwood Dowel, ⅜" .... 2"
Hardwood Toy Wheel, ¾" diameter ... 1 each
Hardwood Toy Wheels, 2" diameter .. 4 each
Carpenter's Glue .... Small container
Non-toxic varnish or paint of several colors in
　small containers

Cutting List

Part 1 ... Chassis .... Make 1
Part 2 ... Engine Hood .... Make 1
Part 3 ... Rear Body .... Make 1
Part 4 ... Door .... Make 2
Part 5 ... Right Fender .... Make 1
Part 6 ... Left Fender .... Make 1
Part 7 ... Fender Side .... Make 2
Part 8 ... Seat .... Make 2
Part 9 ... Convertible Top Boot ... Make 1
Part 10 .. Headlight .... Make 2

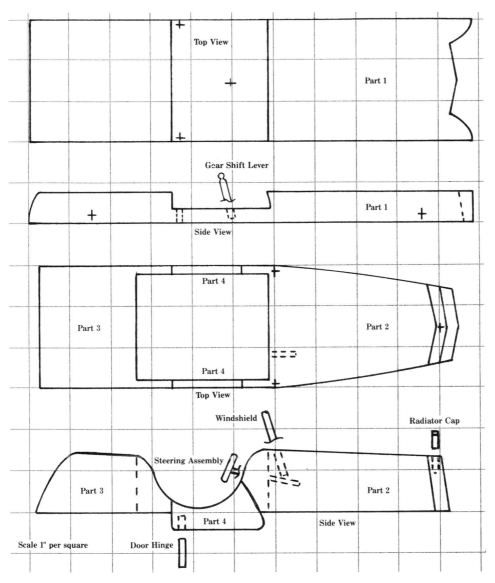

Illus. 80   Layout of parts. 1938 Jaguar.

Instructions

LAYOUT

1. Lay out the chassis (Part 1), two doors (Part 4), the fenders (Parts 5 and 6), two fender sides (Part 7), and the convertible top boot (Part 9) on the ¾″ hardwood stock (Illus. 80 and 81).

2. Lay out the engine hood (Part 2), the rear body (Part 3), and the two seats (Part 8) (Illus. 80 and 81).

3. Use your band saw or jigsaw to cut these parts to shape (Illus. 82).

4. The headlights (Part 10) are to be shaped from ⅜″ dowel stock (Illus. 81).

5. These parts should now be shaped and detailed as desired to prepare them for assembly (Illus. 82).

ASSEMBLY

6. Drill the axle holes into the chassis (Part 1) (Illus. 80).

7. Locate and drill all ⅛″ holes needed for installation of the steering column, the gearshift, the radiator cap, and the windshield (Illus. 80).

8. Drill the 9⁄64″ hinge mounting holes into the floor of the chassis (Illus. 80).

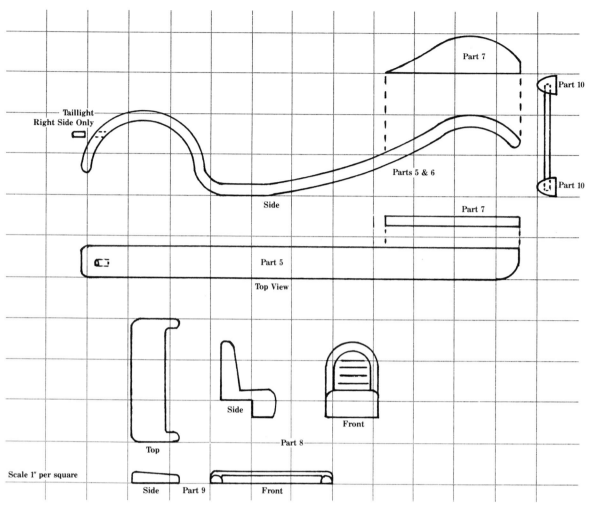

Taillight
Right Side Only

Part 7

Part 10

Part 10

Parts 5 & 6

Side

Part 7

Part 5

Top View

Top

Side

Front

Side

Part 8

Part 9

Front

Scale 1″ per square

Illus. 81   Parts. 1938 Jaguar.

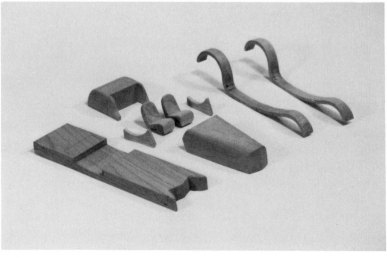

Illus. 82   Cut the parts to shape.

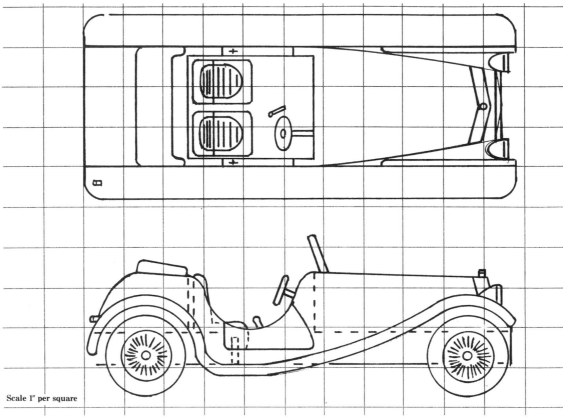

Scale 1″ per square

Illus. 83   Final assembly, 1938 Jaguar.

Illus. 84

9. Drill ⅛″ holes into the bottoms of the doors, for hinge mounting.

10. Glue short pieces of ⅛″ dowel sections, approximately ¾″ in length, into the hinge mounting holes in the doors.

11. To secure the doors in place, simply insert the hinge pins into the mounting holes in the chassis drilled for that purpose.

12. Position the engine hood (Part 2) and the rear body (Part 3) into place on the chassis.

Allow enough room around the door area to prevent restriction of door movement. You may find it helpful to sand and round the hinged sides of the doors, to improve door operation.

13. Position the fender sides (Part 7) into place on the insides of the fenders (Parts 5 and 6), and secure in place with glue (Illus. 81).

14. Align the fender assemblies to the sides of the car's body and glue in place (Illus. 83).

15. Using ⅛″ dowel sections, as shown, install

the steering shaft, the radiator cap, and the windshield (Illus. 80 and 84).

16. Attach the ¾″ diameter hardwood toy wheel, to serve as a steering wheel, to the end of the steering shaft (Illus. 83).

17. Glue the seats (Part 8) and the convertible top boot (Part 9) into place (Illus. 83).

18. Mount the headlights, as indicated in Illus. 81, 83, and 84, by gluing them between the two fenders.

19. Paint or varnish your project.

20. Install the 2″ hardwood toy wheels (Illus. 83 and 84).

21. Your Classic 1938 Jaguar is now complete.

1957 Triumph TR-5

Illus. 85

Materials List

Hardwood Stock, ¾″	*5″ × 25″*
Hardwood Block .... *2″ × 3″ × 12″*	
Hardwood Dowel, ⅛″	*10″*
Hardwood Dowel, ¼″	*18″*
Hardwood Dowel, ⅜″	*2″*
Hardwood Toy Wheel, ¾″ diameter ...	*1 each*
Hardwood Toy Wheels, 2″ diameter ..	*4 each*
Carpenter's Glue	*Small container*
Non-toxic varnish or several colors of paint in small containers	

Cutting List

Part 1	*... Chassis*	*Make 1*
Part 2	*... Engine Hood*	*Make 1*
Part 3	*... Rear Body*	*Make 1*
Part 4	*... Door*	*Make 2*
Part 5	*... Right Fender*	*Make 1*
Part 6	*... Left Fender*	*Make 1*
Part 7	*... Seat*	*Make 2*
Part 8	*... Convertible Top Boot* ...	*Make 1*
Part 9	*... Bumper*	*Make 2*
Part 10	*.. Headlight*	*Make 2*

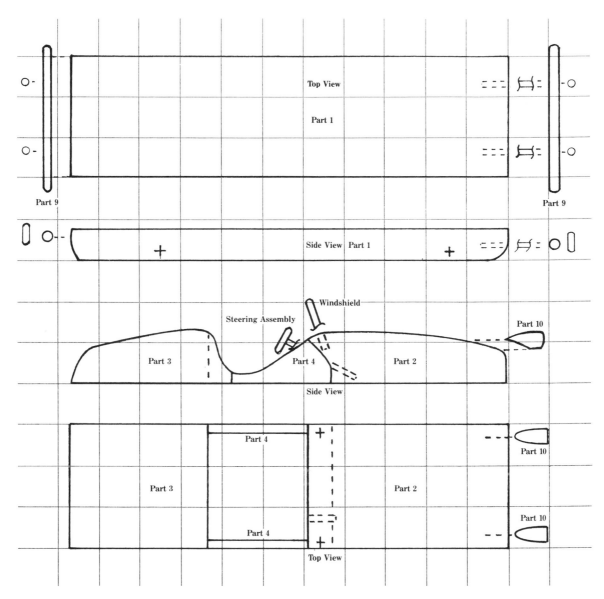

Illus. 86   Layout of parts. 1957 Triumph.

Instructions

LAYOUT

1. Lay out the chassis (Part 1), two doors (Part 4), the fenders (Parts 5 and 6), and the convertible top boot (Part 8) on the ¾″ hardwood stock (Illus. 86 and 87).

2. Lay out the engine hood (Part 2), the rear body (Part 3), and the two seats (Part 7) on the hardwood block material (Illus. 86 and 87).

3. Cut these parts to shape with your band saw or jigsaw (Illus. 88).

4. Make the headlights (Part 10) by shaping ⅜″ diameter dowel sections (Illus. 86).

5. All of these parts should now be shaped and detailed as desired in preparation for assembly.

ASSEMBLY

6. Drill the correct-sized axle holes into the chassis (Part 1).

7. Locate and drill the ⅛″ holes, as indicated,

for mounting the steering column, the bumpers, and the windshield post (Illus. 86).

8. Position the engine hood (Part 1), the doors (Part 4), and the rear body (Part 3) into place on the chassis (Part 1), and secure in place with carpenter's glue.

> **NOTE:** These doors are not operative and should be glued into place (Illus. 89).

9. Glue the fenders (Parts 5 and 6) into place on the sides of the body assembly (Illus. 89 and 90).

10. The front and rear bumpers (Part 9) are identical and are made from ¼″ diameter dowel sections. The front bumper is mounted in a protruded position by using ⅛″ dowel sections as the protruding supports (Illus. 86, 89, and 90). The rear bumper is to be mounted directly to the rear of the body assembly with glue. The vertical bumper guards are short sections of ⅛″ dowel simply glued in place (Illus. 90).

11. Using ⅛″ dowel sections, construct the steering column and windshield, and glue in place (Illus. 86 and 90).

12. Glue the ¾″ diameter hardwood toy wheel to the steering column.

13. Glue the seats (Part 7) and the convertible top boot (Part 8) in place.

14. Glue the headlights (Part 10) in place (Illus. 89).

15. Paint the entire vehicle at this time.

16. Mount the 2″ diameter hardwood toy wheels.

17. Your new 1957 Triumph TR-5 is now finished. Enjoy displaying it.

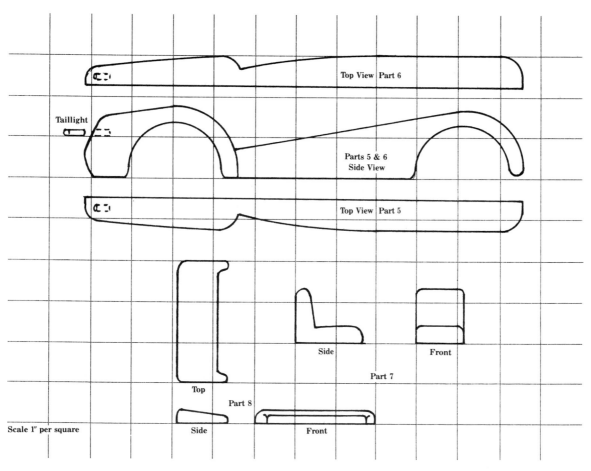

Illus. 87   Parts. 1957 Triumph.

Illus. 88   Cut parts to shape using a band saw or jigsaw.

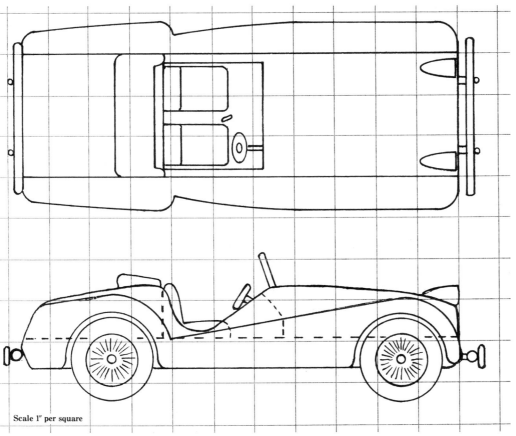

Illus. 89   Final assembly, 1957 Triumph.

Scale 1″ per square

Illus. 90

Duesenberg SSJ

1925 Model "T" Ford

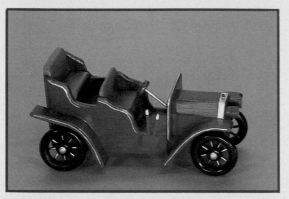

1903 Fiat

1938 Jaguar SS-100

Stutz Bearcat

1910 Cadillac

B

1965 Ford Mustang Convertible

1988 Corvette Convertible

Ferrari Formula Track Racer

Pikes Peak Racing Vehicle

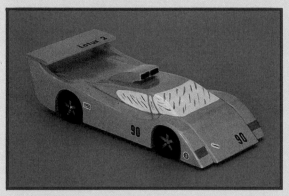

Lotus Formula Roadracer

Drag Racer

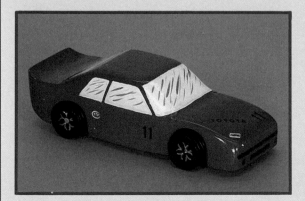

Toyota Stock Racing Car

Porsche Formula Track Racer

U.S. Forest Ranger

4 × 4 Pickup

4 × 4 Toyota

· 5 ·
MODERN EUROPEAN SPORTS CARS

The European Sports Car of Today has emerged from a heritage of many years of automotive engineering and manufacturing. It has been purposefully designed to be the fastest, safest, and most dazzling automobile in the world. To own this car is to say to the world, "I am part of the *haut monde*. Take notice of me." To drive this car is to leave the world of reality behind and step into a new existence in which man and machine become one, in which the road becomes an extension of one's body.

Building the cars in this chapter brings with it a certain amount of excitement. Their very designs and styles are exciting; consequently, they make wonderful projects for the woodworker in his teens. To those who will be supervising a young woodworker: Remember shop safety. Be sure that he or she knows how to operate your power tools safely.

1988 Lamborghini Countach

Illus. 91

Materials List

Hardwood Stock, ¾" .... 5" × 15"
Hardwood Block .... 2½" × 3" × 11"
Hardwood Dowel, ¼" .... 10"
Hardwood Toy Wheels, 1½" diameter . 4 each
Carpenter's Glue .... Small container
Non-toxic varnish or two or three colors of
   paint in small containers

Cutting List

Part 1 ... Body Center Section ... Make 1
Part 2 ... Right Body Side
            Section .... Make 1
Part 3 ... Left Body Side Section . Make 1
Part 4 ... Spoiler Support .... Make 2
Part 5 ... Spoiler .... Make 1
Part 6 ... Air Scoop .... Make 2

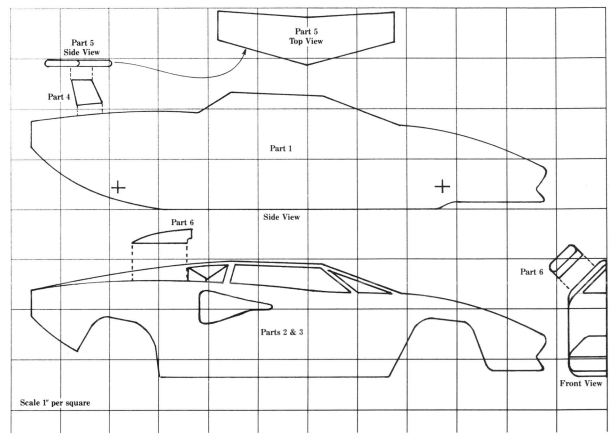

Illus. 92   Layout of parts. 1988 Lamborghini.

Instructions

LAYOUT

1. Use the block of hardwood to lay out the body center section (Part 1) (Illus. 92 and 93).

2. Lay out the right and left body side sections (Parts 2 and 3), the spoiler (Part 5), two spoiler supports (Part 4), and two air scoops (Part 6) on the ¾" hardwood stock (Illus. 92).

3. Use your band saw or jigsaw to cut these parts to shape (Illus. 94).

4. Sand and shape these parts as desired to prepare them for assembly.

> **NOTE:** The body side sections should be sanded quite a bit near the tops, as shown in the front view of Illus. 92. This will bestow on the model a realistic and streamlined appearance.

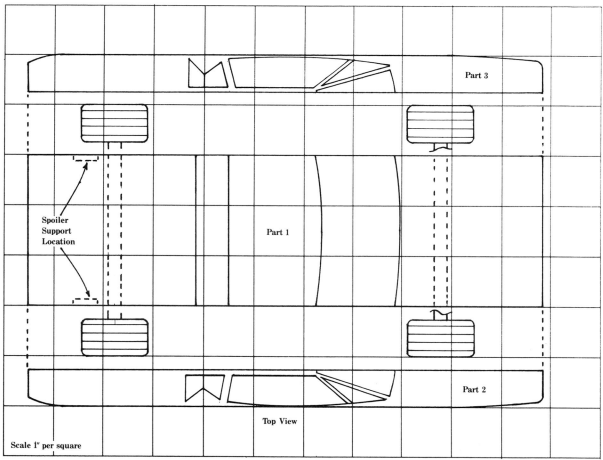

Part 3

Spoiler
Support
Location

Part 1

Part 2

Top View

Scale 1″ per square

Illus. 93   Parts. 1988 Lamborghini.

Illus. 94   Cut parts to shape.

Illus. 95   Complete body assembly for Lamborghini.

ASSEMBLY

5. Drill the two axle holes through the body center section (Part 1) (Illus. 92).

6. Align and glue the right and left body side sections (Parts 2 and 3) in place at the sides of the center section (Illus. 93).

7. Position and glue the two spoiler supports (Part 4) in place, as indicated in Illus. 93.

8. Align and glue the spoiler (Part 5) in place.

9. Position and glue the two air scoops (Part 6) as indicated (Illus. 92 and 95).

10. Paint the entire project at this time. Remember that an impressive amount of detail can be achieved through the careful use of paint.

11. Install the four 1½″ diameter hardwood toy wheels.

12. This 1988 Lamborghini Countach is now complete and ready for display or use.

1988 Lotus Esprit Turbo

Illus. 96

Materials List

Hardwood Stock, ¾" .... *5" × 10"*
Hardwood Block .... *2¼" × 2½" × 10"*
Hardwood Dowel, ¼" .... *10"*
Hardwood Toy Wheels, 1½" diameter . *4 each*
Carpenter's Glue .... *Small container*
*Non-toxic varnish or several colors of paint in
     small containers*

Cutting List

Part 1 ... *Body Center Section* ... *Make 1*
Part 2 ... *Right Body Side
                 Section* .... *Make 1*
Part 3 ... *Left Body Side Section* . *Make 1*

Instructions

LAYOUT

1. Lay out the body center section (Part 1) on the hardwood block (Illus. 97 and 98).

2. Lay out the two body side sections (Parts 2 and 3) on the ¾" hardwood stock (Illus. 97 and 98).

3. Using a band saw or jigsaw, cut each of these parts to shape (Illus. 99).

4. Sand, shape, and detail as desired, to make these parts ready for assembly.

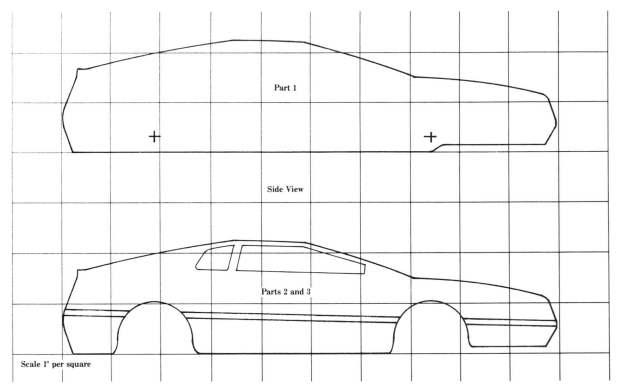

Part 1

Side View

Parts 2 and 3

Scale 1″ per square

Illus. 97   Layout of parts for the Lotus Turbo.

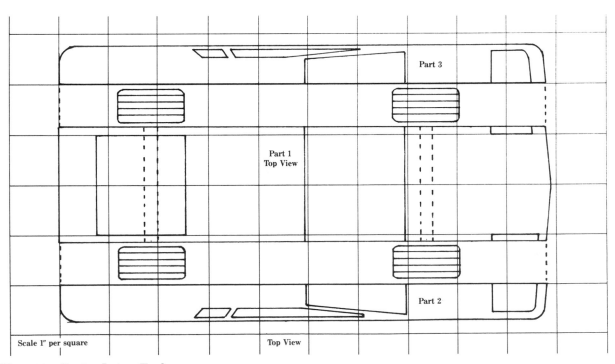

Part 3

Part 1
Top View

Part 2

Scale 1″ per square

Top View

Illus. 98   Parts. Lotus Turbo.

ASSEMBLY

5. Align and glue the two body side sections to the center section.

6. Paint or varnish the assembled project.

7. Install the four 1½″ hardwood toy wheels to complete the assembly.

8. The Lotus Turbo is complete and ready for use.

Illus. 99   Using a band saw or jigsaw, cut parts to shape.

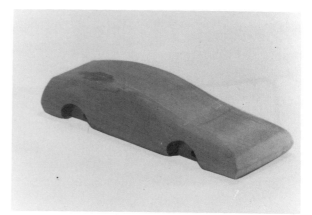

Illus. 100   Sand and shape for added authenticity.

1988 Ferrari 328

Illus. 101

Materials List

Hardwood Stock, ¾" .... *5" × 10"*
Hardwood Block .... *2" × 2" × 10"*
Hardwood Dowel, ¼" .... *10"*
Hardwood Toy Wheels, 1½" .... *4 each*
Carpenter's Glue .... *Small container*
*Non-toxic varnish or paint in several colors in
    small containers*

Cutting List

Part 1 ... Body Center Section ... Make 1
*Part 2 ... Left Body Side
        Section* .... *Make 1*
*Part 3 ... Right Body Side
        Section* .... *Make 1*

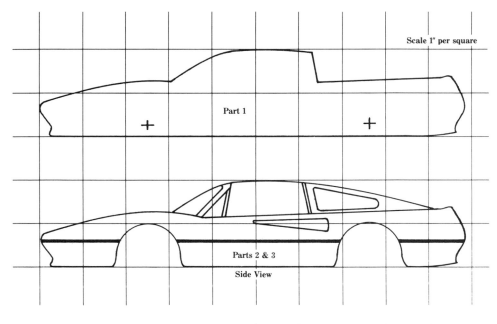

*Illus. 102   Layout of
parts. 1988 Ferrari
328.*

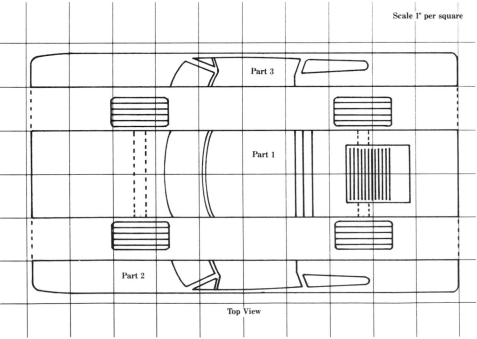

*Illus. 103   Layout of
parts.*

Instructions

LAYOUT

1. Lay out the body center section (Part 1) on the hardwood block (Illus. 102 and 103).

2. Lay out the two body side sections (Parts 2 and 3) on the ¾" hardwood stock (Illus. 102 and 103).

3. Use your band saw or jigsaw to cut these parts to shape (Illus. 104).

4. Shape, detail, and sand as desired to prepare these parts for assembly (Illus. 104).

ASSEMBLY

5. Align and glue the two body side sections to the center section.

6. Paint or varnish the project.

7. Install the four 1½" hardwood toy wheels to complete the assembly.

8. Your Ferrari 328 is now complete.

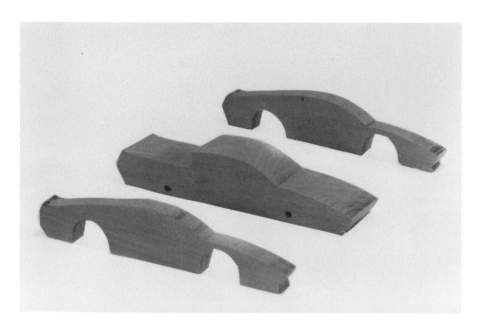

Illus. 104 The 1988 Ferrari 328 has only three major parts.

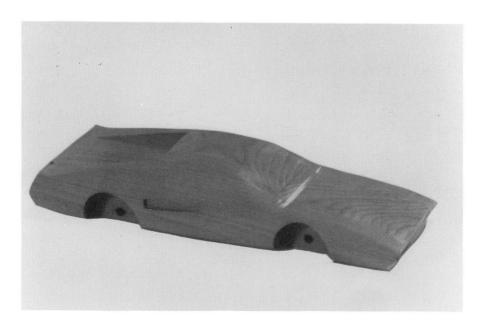

Illus. 105 Complete body assembly with shaping work done.

· 6 ·
U.S. SPORTS CARS

As the Europeans channelled a great deal of energy and talent into developing the ultimate sports car, the U.S. auto manufacturers settled down to meeting the needs of the general public. After all, it is a bit impractical for Mother to deliver three kids to school, take the family dog to the vet, and bring home seven bags of groceries in a Lamborghini, even though she might really love doing so. However, U.S. engineers, too, have grown to be among the best in the world. The automobiles they have developed are stylish, reliable, and quite luxurious at times. They are the finest in the market for which they were developed. There has been an occasion or two, though, when the U.S. automotive designer has sat down to his drawing table with a coffee cup in his hand and a gleam in his eye and thought, "Today I'm going to do something different." And do something different he did. He revolutionized U.S. automotive history. American-built sports cars have become classics in their own right and still today are some of the most sought-after automobiles in the world.

One of these projects would make a great gift to someone who actually owns one of the "Classic American Sports Cars."

1965 Ford Mustang Convertible

Illus. 106

Materials List

Hardwood Stock, ¾" .... *5" × 30"*
Hardwood Block .... *2" × 3" × 15"*
Hardwood Dowel, 1/16" .... *3"*
Hardwood Dowel, ⅛" .... *8"*
Hardwood Dowel, ¼" .... *10"*
Hardwood Dowel, ½" .... *5"*
Hardwood Dowel, 1" .... *2"*
Hardwood Toy Wheels, 1¾" diameter . 4 each
Carpenter's Glue .... *Small container*
Non-toxic varnish or two or three colors of
   paint in small containers

Cutting List

Part 1 ... *Chassis* .... *Make 1*
Part 2 ... *Engine Hood* .... *Make 1*
Part 3 ... *Rear Body* .... *Make 1*
Part 4 ... *Right Body Side*
                Section .... *Make 1*
Part 5 ... *Left Body Side Section* . *Make 1*
Part 6 ... *Windshield Crossbar* ... *Make 1*
Part 7 ... *Convertible Top Boot* ... *Make 1*
Part 8 ... *Front Bucket Seat* ..... *Make 2*
Part 9 ... *Rear Bench Seat* .... *Make 1*
Part 10 .. *Steering Wheel* .... *Make 1*
Part 11 .. *Rear Bumper* .... *Make 1*
Part 12 .. *Front Bumper* .... *Make 1*
Part 13 .. *Transmission Tunnel* ... *Make 1*
Part 14 .. *Taillight* .... *Make 2*
Part 15 .. *Grill Bar* .... *Make 1*

Instructions

LAYOUT

1. Lay out the chassis (Part 1), the two body side sections (Parts 4 and 5), the windshield crossbar (Part 6), the convertible top boot (Part 7), the front and rear bumpers (Parts 11 and 12), the two taillights (Part 14), and the grill bar (Part 5) on the ¾" hardwood stock (Illus. 107, 109, and 111).

2. Lay out the engine hood (Part 2), the rear body (Part 3), the two front bucket seats (Part 8), and one rear bench seat (Part 9) on the hardwood block material (Illus. 108, 110, and 111).

3. Use your band saw or jigsaw to cut all of these parts to shape (Illus. 112).

4. The transmission tunnel (Part 13) is made from a section of ½" dowel; one side is sanded away to create a semi-cylindrical shape (Illus. 107).

5. The steering wheel (Part 10) is shaped from a section of 1" dowel (Illus. 111).

6. Shape, detail, and sand each part to prepare it for assembly.

NOTE: With this project, the shaping will have a great deal of bearing upon the authenticity of the finished product; therefore, take your time and give your full attention to this portion of the work.

ASSEMBLY

7. Drill the axle holes into the chassis (Part 1) (Illus. 107).

8. Shape the transmission tunnel (Part 13) so that it will fit properly into the recess of the floor area of the chassis (Part 1), and glue it in place (Illus. 107).

9. Drill the ⅛" hole for mounting the gearshift in the transmission tunnel, as shown in Illus. 107.

10. Make the gearshift lever from a short section of ⅛" dowel by shaping one end with sandpaper, to bring about the appearance of a ball for the shifting handle.

11. Glue the gearshift lever into the hole in the transmission tunnel (Illus. 107).

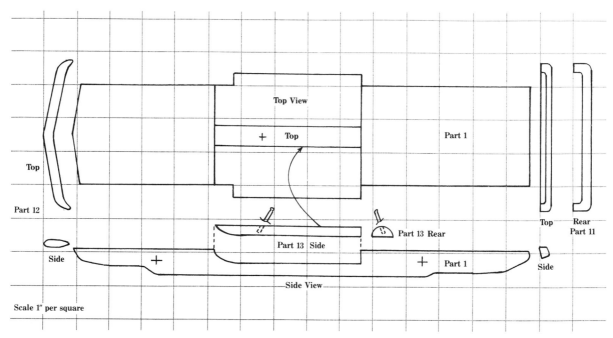

Illus. 107   Layout of parts. 1965 Ford Mustang.

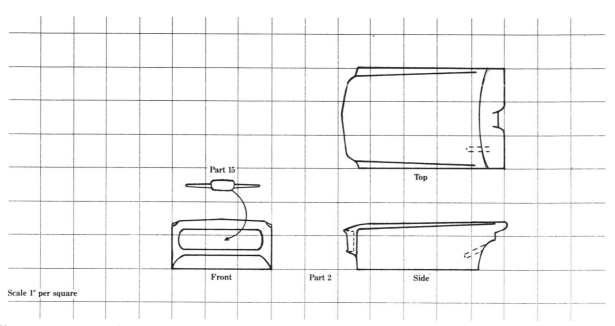

Illus. 108   Layout of parts.

12. Position the engine hood (Part 2), the rear body (Part 3), and the two body side sections (Parts 4 and 5) on the chassis (Part 1) simultaneously so that the best alignment can be obtained, and glue them all in place (Illus. 113).

13. Drill ⅛″ holes for mounting the steering column and windshield post (Illus. 108 and 109).

14. Drill a ¼″ hole into the center of the rear body for mounting the gas cap (Illus. 110).

15. The gas cap is a short section of ¼″ dowel inserted into the mounting hole, and extending

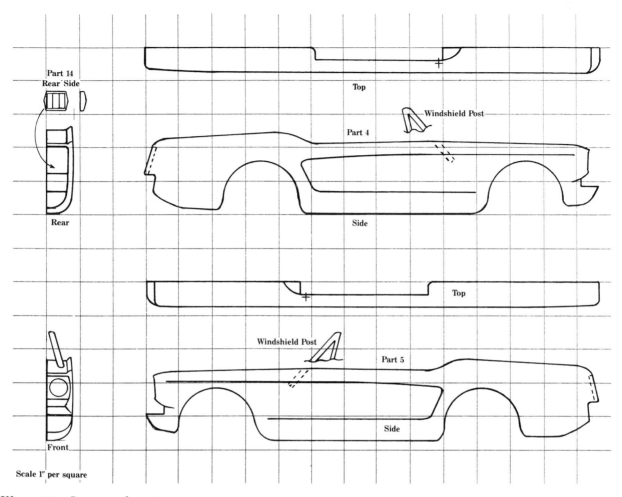

Illus. 109   Layout of parts.

about 1/16″ beyond the surface of the rear body.

16. Glue the seats (Parts 8 and 9) in place (Illus. 113).

17. Glue the convertible top boot (Part 7) in place (Illus. 113).

18. Drill a 1/8″ hole into the center of the pointed end of the steering wheel (Part 10), and, using a 1/8″ dowel section approximately 2″ long, glue the steering assembly in place (Illus. 113).

19. Install the 1/8″ dowel sections for the windshield post (Illus. 109, 113, and 115).

20. Make the small window posts that join the windshield post from 1/16″ dowel and glue them in place.

21. Glue the windshield crossbar (Part 6) in place (Illus. 113 and 114).

22. Glue the taillights (Part 14) in place (Illus. 109 and 114).

23. Glue the front and rear bumpers (Parts 11 and 12) in place (Illus. 113, 114, and 115).

24. Glue the bar grill (Part 15) in place (Illus. 108).

25. Paint or varnish the entire project.

26. Install the 1¾″ diameter toy wheels to complete the assembly.

27. You are now the proud owner of a "Classic 1965 Ford Mustang Convertible," a true collector's item.

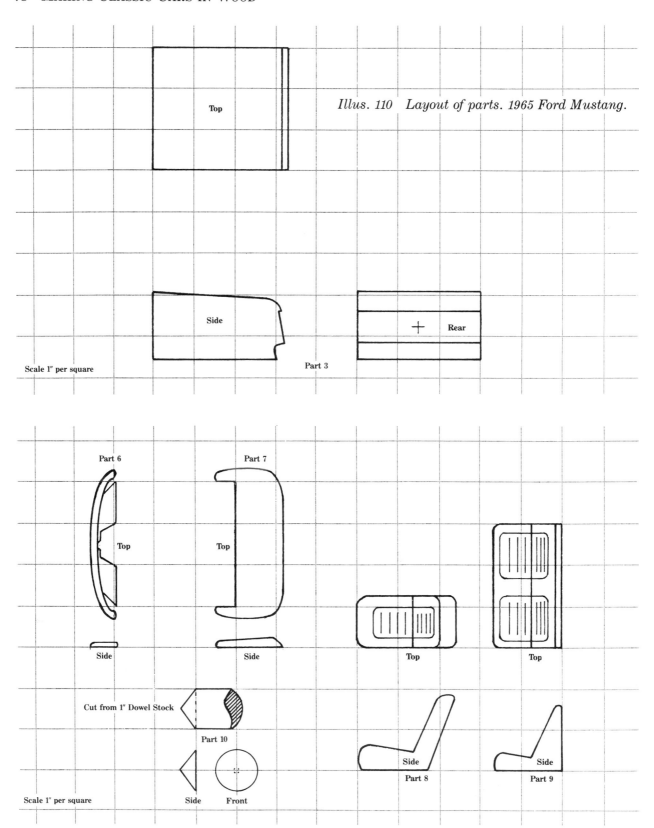

Illus. 110   Layout of parts. 1965 Ford Mustang.

Illus. 111   Parts.

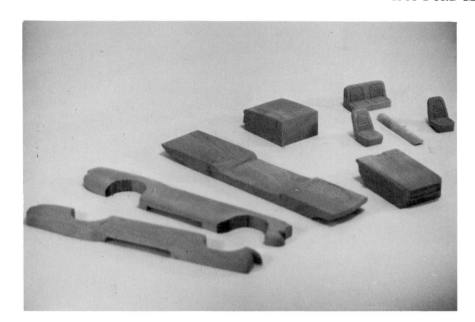

Illus. 112   Use your band saw to cut parts to shape.

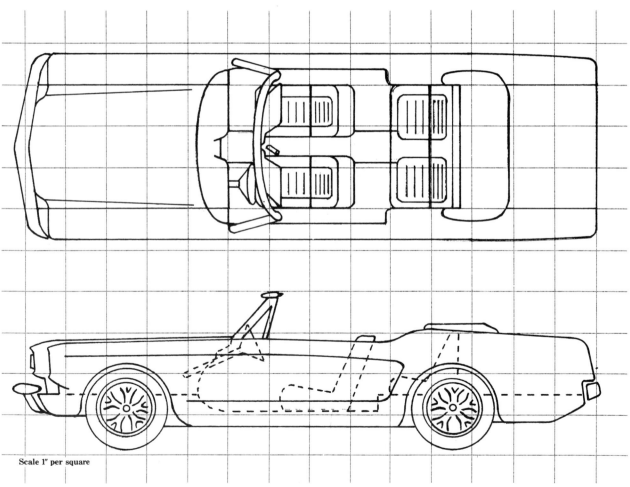

Scale 1″ per square

Illus. 113   Assembly details.

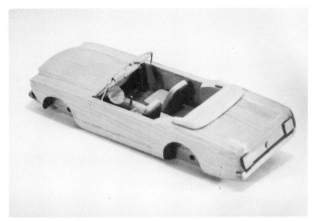

Illus. 114   Note the detail of the taillights, gas cap, and rear bumper.

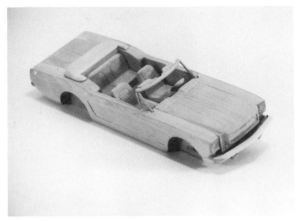

Illus. 115   With this project, the shaping will have a great deal of bearing upon the authenticity of the finished project.

1988 Corvette Convertible

Illus. 116

Materials List

Hardwood Stock, ¾" .... 5" × 32"
Hardwood Block .... 2½" × 3" × 15"
Hardwood Dowel, ⅛" .... 10"
Hardwood Dowel, ¼" .... 10"
Hardwood Toy Wheels, 2¼" diameter . 4 each
Carpenter's Glue .... Small container
Non-toxic varnish or two or three colors of
   paint in small containers

Cutting List

Part 1 ... Chassis .... Make 1
Part 2 ... Engine Hood .... Make 1
Part 3 ... Rear Body .... Make 1
Part 4 ... Right Body Side
               Section .... Make 1
Part 5 ... Left Body Side Section . Make 1
Part 6 ... Windshield Crossbar ... Make 1
Part 7 ... Steering Wheel .... Make 1
Part 8 ... Bucket Seat .... Make 2

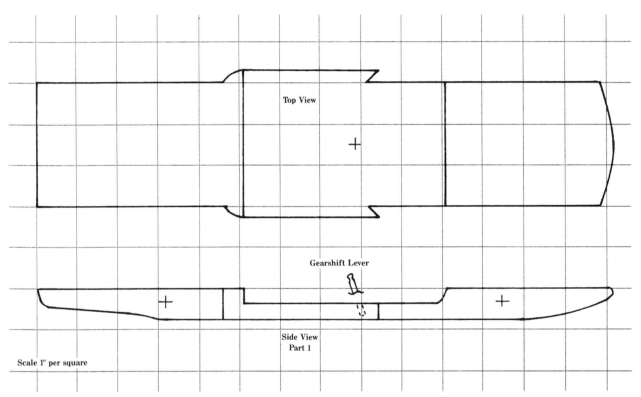

Illus. 117   Layout of parts. 1988 Corvette Convertible.

Instructions

LAYOUT

1. Lay out the chassis (Part 1), the right and left body side sections (Parts 4 and 5), and the windshield crossbar (Part 6) on the ¾" hardwood stock (Illus. 117, 120, and 121).

2. Lay out the engine hood (Part 2), the rear body (Part 3), and the two bucket seats (Part 8) on the hardwood block material (Illus. 118, 119, and 121).

3. The steering wheel (Part 7) can be made by shaping the end of a 1" diameter dowel and then cutting off the access (Illus. 121).

4. Use your band saw or jigsaw to cut each of these parts to shape (Illus. 122).

5. Sand, shape, and detail each of these parts to prepare them for assembly.

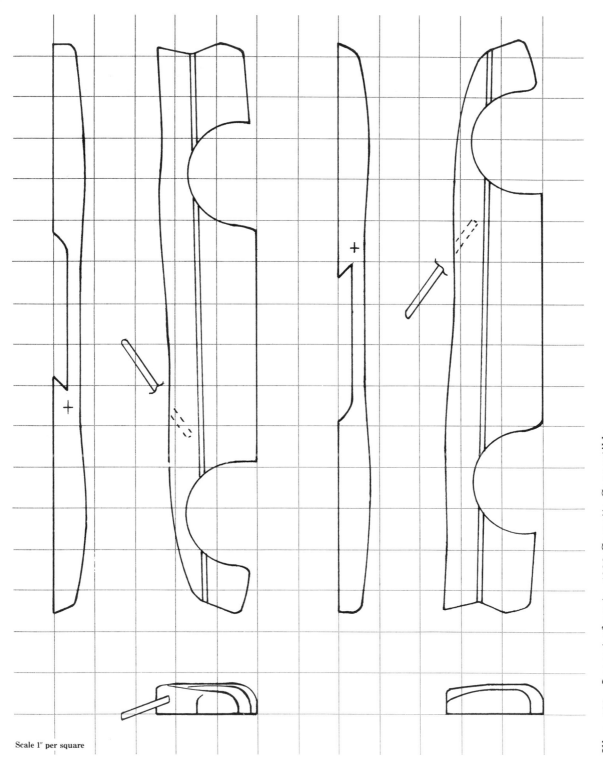

Scale 1″ per square

Illus. 120 Layout of parts. 1988 Corvette Convertible.

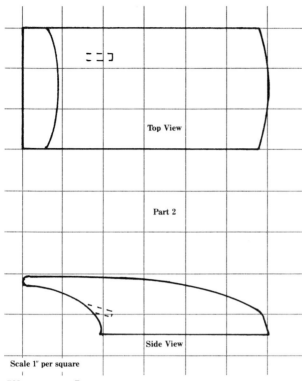

Illus. 118 Layout.

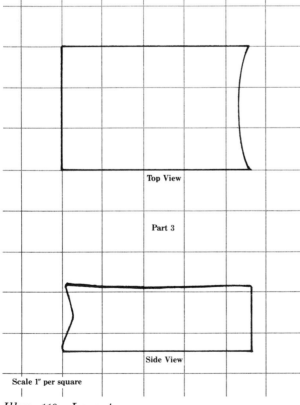

Illus. 119 Layout.

ASSEMBLY

6. Drill the axle holes in the chassis (Part 1) (Illus. 117).

7. Drill the ⅛″ mounting holes for the steering column, the gearshift, and the windshield post (Illus. 117, 118, and 120).

8. Make the gearshift lever from a section of ⅛″ dowel by shaping one end with sandpaper, to bring about the appearance of a ball for the shifting handle (Illus. 117).

9. Insert the gearshift lever into the hole in the chassis and secure with glue (Illus. 117).

10. Position the engine hood (Part 2), the rear body (Part 3), and both body side sections (Parts 4 and 5) on the chassis (Part 1) simultaneously so that the proper alignment can be obtained, and glue in place (Illus. 124).

11. Glue the seats (Part 8) into position (Illus. 124).

12. Drill a ⅛″ hole into the pointed end of the steering wheel (Part 7).

13. Using a section of ⅛″ dowel as the steering column, glue the steering assembly into place (Illus. 124).

14. Install the ⅛″ dowel section for the windshield post (Illus. 124 and 125).

15. Glue the windshield crossbar into position on the windshield post (Illus. 124 and 125).

16. The entire project can now be finished with non-toxic paint or varnish to suit your taste.

17. Install the 2¼″ diameter hardwood wheels to complete the car.

18. This is a 1988 Corvette Convertible, destined to become a classic. Enjoy your new model.

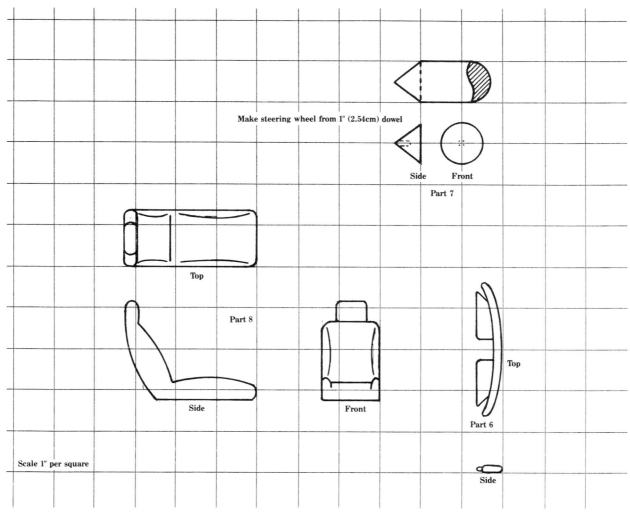

Make steering wheel from 1″ (2.54cm) dowel

Side   Front

Part 7

Top

Part 8

Side

Front

Top

Part 6

Side

Scale 1″ per square

Illus. 121   Layout.

Illus. 122   Use your band saw to cut the parts to shape.

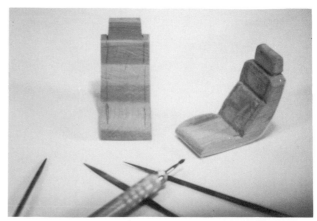

Illus. 123   Detail of the aircraft-type bucket seats for the Corvette.

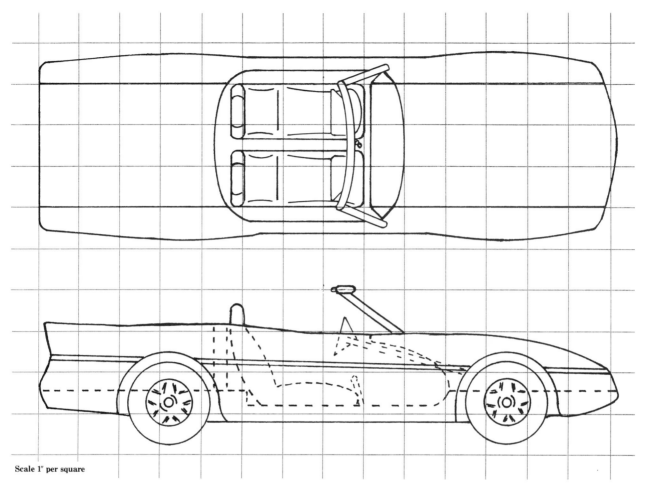

Scale 1″ per square

Illus. 124   Completed assembly, 1988 Corvette Convertible.

Illus. 125   Windshield crossbar is glued into position.

· 7 ·

EUROPEAN ROAD RACING

The four-wheeled vehicle that we know as the motorcar has been developed in various ways in different parts of the world. For some it has become an invaluable tool by which and with which they operate and manage their very lives. To some it is an expensive toy. To some a status symbol, purchased and maintained for the sole purpose of impressing their neighbors and other onlookers. To many today it is a livelihood; some members of this group spend their time repairing the darn things for the rest of us, for instance. And, yes, there are always those who possess the competitive spirit: the ones who feel perpetually compelled to pit their strength or skill against that of their fellow men. After all, what would life be without competition?

The contest of European Road Racing over the past fourscore years has literally been elevated to a science. In the earlier days it was merely that: a contest. European Road Racing was a contest to determine which driver could best command his skills to drive his car over a pre-determined course in the shortest time—allowing, of course, that his car would hold together long enough to accomplish this task.

Today, the concept is about the same; however, the cars are a bit different. A racing car is designed and built for no other purpose than to be faster than the next one. It has been designed to maintain the fastest possible speed, whether travelling in a straight line or around the worst of hairpin curves. The engine, the tires, the brakes, the aerodynamic shape—every aspect of its design has been forged with this single focus in mind.

The next projects are incredibly simple to build. They have only a few parts, and the compound shapes are not difficult to master. Either of them would be a good project for one of those Saturday afternoons when your favorite team is behind 0 to 33 at the half.

Jaguar Formula Roadracer

Materials List

Hardwood Stock, ¾" .... 4" × 16"
Hardwood Block .... 2½" × 3" × 11"
Hardwood Dowel, ¼" .... 20"
Hardwood Toy Wheels, 1½" .... 4 each
Carpenter's Glue .... Small container
Non-toxic varnish or two or three colors of paint in small containers

Cutting List

Part 1 ... Body Center Section ... Make 1
Part 2 ... Left Body Side Section . Make 1
Part 3 ... Right Body Side Section .... Make 1
Part 4 ... Spoiler .... Make 1

Illus. 126

Instructions

LAYOUT

1. Lay out the two body side sections (Parts 2 and 3) and the spoiler (Part 4) on the ¾″ hardwood stock (Illus. 127).

2. Lay out the body center section (Part 1) on the hardwood block material (Illus. 127).

3. Cut these parts to shape with your band saw or jigsaw.

4. Sand, shape, and detail all of these parts to prepare them for assembly.

ASSEMBLY

5. Drill the two axle holes through the body center section (Part 1) (Illus. 127).

6. Drill the eight ¼″ holes into the top of the body center section (Part 1) to a depth of ¼″ (Illus. 127).

7. Align and glue the two body side sections (Parts 2 and 3) in place to the sides of the body center section (Part 1) (Illus. 128).

8. Make eight ½″ long sections of dowel from ¼″ diameter dowel stock.

9. Glue the eight short dowel sections into the eight holes at the top of the body center section (Part 1) (Illus. 129).

10. Locate and glue the spoiler (Part 4) in place (Illus. 129).

11. The entire project can now be painted or varnished.

12. Install the 1½″ diameter hardwood toy wheels.

13. This completes the Jaguar Formula Roadracer. She is now ready for the big race at LeMans.

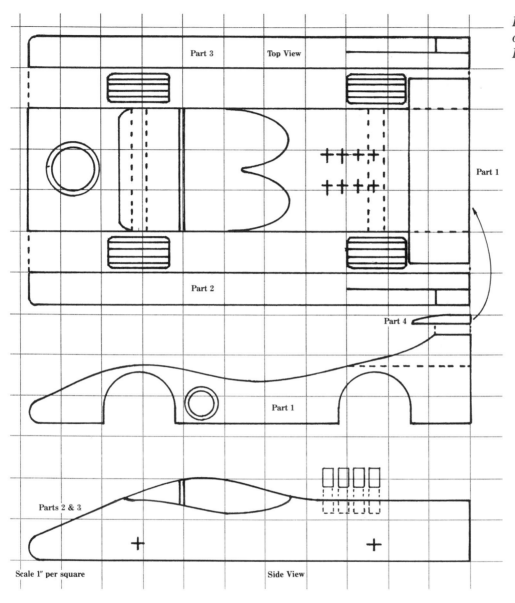

Part 3   Top View

Part 1

Part 2

Part 4

Part 1

Parts 2 & 3

Scale 1″ per square   Side View

Illus. 128   Glue the body side sections to the sides of the center section.

Illus. 129   The simplicity of design is at odds with the realistic appearance.

Lotus Formula Roadracer

Illus. 130

Materials List

Hardwood Stock, ¾" .... 5" × 12"
Hardwood Block .... 2½" × 3" × 12"
Hardwood Dowel, ¼" .... 10"
Hardwood Toy Wheels, 1½" diameter . 4 each
Carpenter's Glue .... Small container
Non-toxic varnish or several colors of paint in
   small containers

Cutting List

Part 1 ... Body Center Section ... Make 1
Part 2 ... Left Body Side Section . Make 1
Part 3 ... Right Body Side
              Section .... Make 1
Part 4 ... Spoiler .... Make 1
Part 5 ... Engine Air Intake
              Scoop .... Make 1

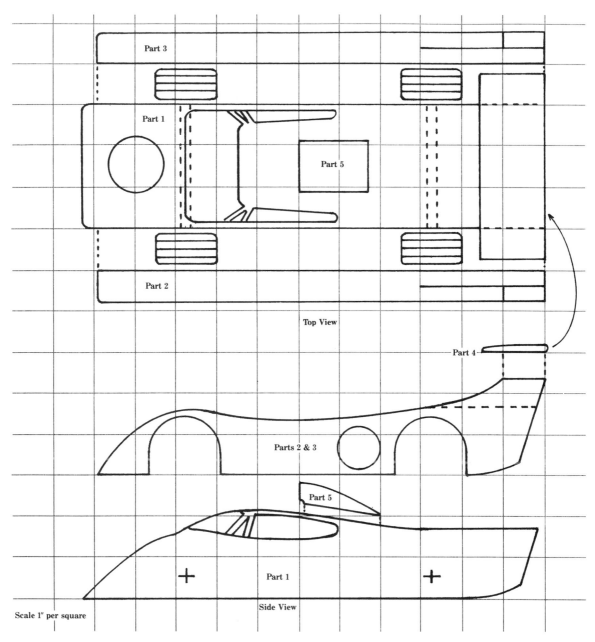

Illus. 131   Layout of parts. Lotus Formula Roadracer.

Instructions

LAYOUT

1. Lay out the two body side sections (Parts 2 and 3), the spoiler (Part 4), and the engine air intake scoop (Part 5) on the ¾″ hardwood stock (Illus. 131).

2. Lay out the body center section (Part 1) on the hardwood block material (Illus. 131).

3. Cut these parts to shape with your band saw or jigsaw (Illus. 132).

4. Sand, shape, and detail these parts, as you desire, to prepare them for assembly (Illus. 132).

Illus. 132   Only four major parts cut to shape with a band saw.

Illus. 133   Lotus Formula Road-racer completed body assembly.

ASSEMBLY

5. Drill the axle holes into the body center section (Part 1), as indicated in Illus. 131.

6. Position the two body side sections (Parts 2 and 3) to the sides of the body center section (Part 1), and secure them with glue (Illus. 131).

7. Secure the spoiler (Part 4) in place with glue (Illus. 131 and 133).

8. Position the engine air intake scoop (Part 5) at the top middle of the body center section (Part 1), and secure in place with glue (Illus. 131 and 133).

9. The entire project is now ready for painting or varnishing, as you desire.

10. Install the 1½″ diameter hardwood toy wheels with the correct-sized axles (Illus. 131).

11. The Lotus Formula Roadracing Machine is now complete.

· 8 ·
U.S. TRACK RACING

The day is May 30, Memorial Day; the time, 5:30 A.M.; the place, Indianapolis, Indiana. The morning is still and silent with the fading of the night. The last few moments of quiet and peacefulness lie over the city. Yet, it is an uneasy peacefulness. The city's inhabitants know full well that today a great battle will be fought here—and a great victory won.

Every year at this time, they come here to fight this battle again. They do not bring their swords and weapons of war with which to defeat their enemies. They bring instead their strange and wonderful chariots, chariots that look like no others and are pulled by hundreds of spirited horses.

This is the Indianapolis 500.

Ferrari Formula Track Racer

Illus. 134

Materials List

Hardwood Stock, ¾" .... *3" × 6"*
Hardwood Block .... *1½" × 3" × 16"*
Hardwood Dowel, ³⁄₁₆" .... *4"*
Hardwood Dowel, ¼" .... *10"*
Hardwood Dowel, ⁷⁄₁₆" .... *2"*
Hardwood Dowel, ½" .... *6"*
Hardwood Dowel, ¾" .... *2"*
Hardwood Toy Wheels, 1½" diameter . *4 each*
Carpenter's Glue .... *Small container*
Non-toxic varnish or two or three colors of paint in small containers

Cutting List

Part 1 ... *Body Center Section* ... Make 1
Part 2 ... *Left Body Side Section* . Make 1
Part 3 ... *Right Body Side Section* .... Make 1
Part 4 ... *Driver* .... Make 1
Part 5 ... *Driver's Headrest* ...... Make 1
Part 6 ... *Engine Air Intake Scoop* .... Make 1
Part 7 ... *Rear Spoiler Support* ... Make 2
Part 8 ... *Rear Spoiler* .... Make 1
Part 9 ... *Left Forward Spoiler* ... Make 1
Part 10 .. *Right Forward Spoiler* .. Make 1
Part 11 .. *Wheel-to-Body Spacer* .. Make 4

Instructions

LAYOUT

1. Lay out the body center section (Part 1) and the left and right body side sections (Parts 2 and 3) on the hardwood block material (Illus. 135).

2. Locate the axle drilling points for both axles on the body center section (Part 1) (Illus. 135).

NOTE: The drilling operations of the following three steps will produce best results if performed with a drill press; however, if one is not available, take care to drill as straight through the block material as possible. This will help in the alignment of parts later.

3. Using a ¼" drill bit, drill completely through the block at each axle location.

4. Now with a ½" drill bit, redrill the holes on both sides of the block to depths of ¾".

5. Also mark and drill the ⁵⁄₃₂" hole for mounting the forward spoilers (Illus. 135).

6. Lay out the engine air intake scoop (Part 6), the two rear spoiler supports (Part 7), the rear spoiler (Part 8), and the left and right forward spoilers (Parts 9 and 10) on the ¾" hardwood stock material (Illus. 135).

7. Use your band saw or jigsaw to cut all of the above parts to shape (Illus. 136).

8. The driver (Part 4) can be made from ⁷⁄₁₆" diameter dowel stock via the method discussed in Chapter 1 (Illus. 135 and 11).

9. The driver's headrest (Part 5) can be shaped from a ¾" diameter dowel section (Illus. 135).

10. The wheel-to-body spacers (Part 11) are ½" diameter dowel sections cut to lengths of 1" (Illus. 135).

11. Shape, detail, and sand all of the above parts to prepare them for final assembly (Illus. 136).

ASSEMBLY

12. Insert two of the wheel-to-body spacers (Part 11) into the two ½" diameter holes on one side of the body center section (Part 1), and secure there with carpenter's glue. Allow the glue to dry completely before proceeding to the next step.

13. Using a ⁹⁄₃₂" drill bit, backdrill the axle holes from the opposite side of the car body (Illus. 137).

14. Now glue the other wheel-to-body spacers into the ½" holes on the opposite side of the car body. Allow the glue to dry thoroughly

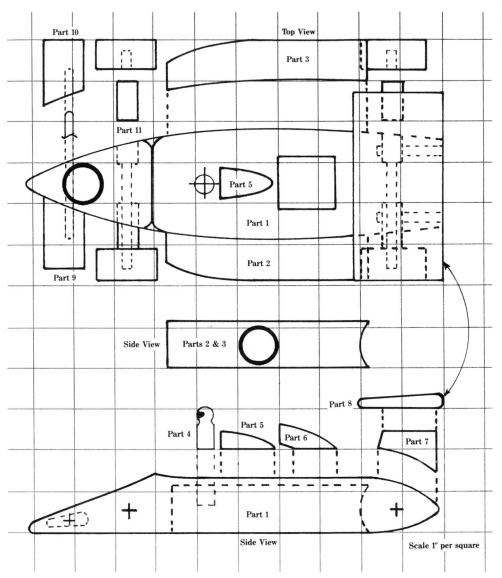

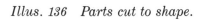

Illus. 135   Layout of parts for the Ferrari Track Racing Indy car.

Illus. 136   Parts cut to shape.

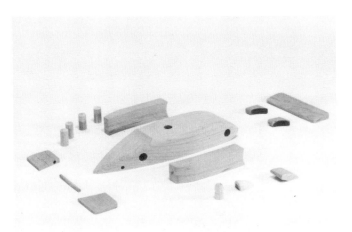

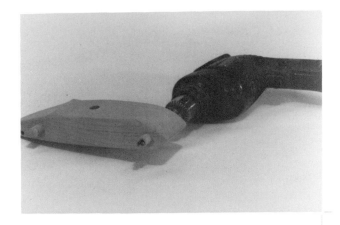

Illus. 137   Backdrill to continue axle holes through spacers.

Illus. 138   Completed assembly of Ferrari Indy Racer.

and backdrill from the other direction. This will complete the axle setup operation.

15. Locate and drill a ¹⁵⁄₃₂″ diameter hole for mounting the driver. Drill to a depth of ½″ (Illus. 135).

16. Position the body side sections (Parts 2 and 3) in place at the sides of the body center section (Part 1), and secure with glue (Illus. 135 and 138).

17. Drill a ³⁄₁₆″ diameter hole into the inside end of each of the forward spoilers (Parts 9 and 10), as shown in Illus. 135 and 136. Drill to a depth of approximately ³⁄₈″.

18. Now, using a ³⁄₁₆″ dowel section approximately 2¼″ long, pin the two forward spoiler halves together through the hole in the forward end of the center body section. Secure all of this assembly into place with carpenter's glue (Illus. 135 and 138).

19. Position the two rear spoiler supports (Part 7) and the rear spoiler (Part 8) at the rear of the body assembly, and secure in place with glue (Illus. 135 and 138).

20. Position the driver's headrest (Part 5) and the engine air intake scoop (Part 6) and secure with glue (Illus. 135 and 138).

21. Paint or varnish the completed assembly and all unassembled parts at this time.

22. Insert the driver (Part 4) into the hole drilled for that purpose, and secure there with glue (Illus. 135 and 138).

23. Install the four 1½″ diameter toy wheels and the ¼″ dowel axles to complete the assembly.

24. The Ferrari Formula Track Racing Car is now complete.

Porsche Formula Track Racer

Illus. 139

Materials List

Hardwood Stock, ¾″	....	*3″ × 6″*
Hardwood Block	....	*2″ × 3″ × 18″*
Hardwood Dowel, ³⁄₁₆″	....	*3″*
Hardwood Dowel, ¼″	....	*15″*
Hardwood Dowel, ⁷⁄₁₆″	....	*2″*
Hardwood Dowel, ½″	....	*6″*
Hardwood Dowel, ¾″	....	*2″*
Hardwood Toy Wheels, 1½″ diameter	.	*4 each*
Carpenter's Glue	....	*Small container*

Non-toxic varnish or two or three colors of paint in small containers

Cutting List

Part 1	...	*Body Center Section*	... *Make 1*
Part 2	...	*Left Body Side Section*	. *Make 1*
Part 3	...	*Right Body Side Section*	.... *Make 1*
Part 4	...	*Driver*	.... *Make 1*
Part 5	...	*Driver's Headrest*	...... *Make 1*
Part 6	...	*Rear Spoiler Support*	... *Make 2*
Part 7	...	*Rear Spoiler*	.... *Make 1*
Part 8	...	*Left Forward Spoiler*	... *Make 1*
Part 9	...	*Right Forward Spoiler*	.. *Make 1*
Part 10	..	*Wheel-to-Body Spacer*	.. *Make 4*

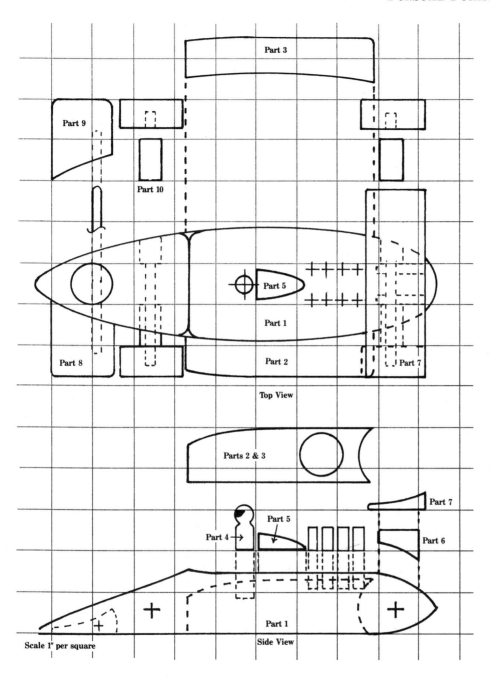

Instructions

LAYOUT

1. Lay out the body section (Part 1), and the left and right body side sections (Parts 2 and 3) on the hardwood block material (Illus. 140).

2. Mark the drilling locations for the two axle holes and the forward spoiler mounting hole (Illus. 140).

NOTE: The drilling operations discussed in the next three steps will produce best results when performed with a drill press; however, if one is not available, take caution to drill as straight through the material as possible. This will help to make the alignment of parts installed in subsequent assembly steps more accurate.

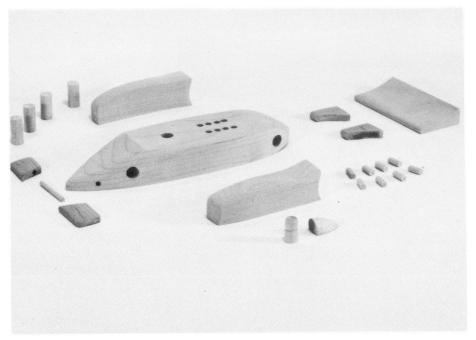

Illus. 141   Cut these parts to shape with your jigsaw.

3. Using a 9/32″ diameter drill bit, drill completely through the block material at each axle location.

4. Now change to a ½″ diameter drill bit, and drill into each axle hole, on both sides of the block, only to a depth of ¾″.

5. With a 5/32″ diameter drill bit, now drill through the block material at the forward spoiler mounting location.

6. Lay out the two rear spoiler supports (Part 6), the rear spoiler (Part 7), and the left and right forward spoilers (Parts 8 and 9) on the ¾″ hardwood stock material (Illus. 140).

7. With a band saw or jigsaw cut all of the above parts to shape (Illus. 141).

8. The driver (Part 4) is to be made from 7/16″ dowel stock, according to the instructions in Chapter 1 (Illus. 140 and 11).

9. The driver's headrest is shaped from a section of ¾″ dowel (Illus. 140 and 141).

10. The eight engine air intake ports are sections of ¼″ dowel, each cut to ½″ in length (Illus. 140 and 141).

11. Make the wheel-to-body spacers (Part 10) by cutting four 1″ sections of ½″ dowel stock (Illus. 140 and 141).

12. To prepare all of the above parts for assembly, all shaping, detailing, and sanding should be done at this time.

ASSEMBLY

13. Insert two of the wheel-to-body spacers (Part 10) into the two ½″ diameter axle holes on one side of the body center section (Part 1), and secure them in place with glue. Allow the glue to dry thoroughly before continuing to the next step.

14. Using a 9/32″ drill bit, backdrill the axle holes from the opposite side of the car body. (Refer to Illus. 137 of the previous project.)

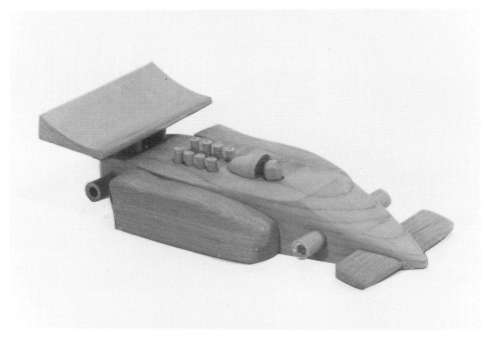

Illus. 142 Porsche Track Racer. Assembly of body completed.

15. Now glue the remaining two wheel-to-body spacers into the ½″ axle holes in the opposite side of the car body. Again, allow the glue to dry completely, and backdrill completely through the entire assembly, completing the axle setup.

16. Drill a ¹⁵⁄₃₂″ hole for installation of the driver. Drill to a depth of ½″ (Illus. 140).

17. Drill the eight holes into the top of the body center section to provide for mounting the engine air intake ports. Make these holes ¼″ in diameter and ¼″ deep.

18. Glue the eight ½″ sections of ¼″ dowel into these holes (Illus. 140 and 142).

19. Position the two body side sections (Parts 2 and 3) in place at the sides of the body center section (Part 1), and secure there with carpenter's glue (Illus. 140 and 142).

20. Drill a ³⁄₁₆″ diameter hole into the inside end of each of the forward spoilers (Parts 8 and 9) (Illus. 140 and 141). Drill these holes to a depth of approximately ⅜″.

21. Now, using a section of ³⁄₁₆″ dowel cut to a length of approximately 2″ as a mounting pin, glue the two halves of the forward spoiler together through the mounting hole in the forward end of the body center section (Illus. 140 and 141).

22. Position the two rear spoiler supports (Part 6) and the rear spoiler (Part 7) at the rear of the body assembly, and secure with glue.

23. Position the driver's headrest just behind the driver mounting hole, and glue in place (Illus. 140 and 142).

24. Paint or varnish, as desired, the completed assembly and all unassembled parts.

25. Insert the driver (Part 4) into the hole provided and secure in place with glue (Illus. 140 and 142).

26. Install the four 1½″ diameter hardwood toy wheels with ¼″ diameter dowel axles.

27. The Porsche Formula Track Racer is now completed.

· 9 ·
STOCK TRACK RACING

When automobile racing first began, it was simply a contest to determine who had the fastest car and/or who was the best driver. The cars used were the same ones being used to provide transportation. In other words, these cars were "stock," or the same as they were when originally built. This "stock car racing" still exists today. Although the cars are not precisely as they were when originally built, they do conform to a set of regulations that allows them to be considered stock cars.

To represent the category of stock car racing in this chapter, cars have been chosen from those manufactured in Japan. Within the past quarter-century, Japanese automobile manufacturers have become major contenders in the automotive industry as well as in the world of auto racing. These projects, too, are quite easy to build. A little attention to detail when shaping and painting either of these will lead to a great display, along with your golfing trophy, on the fireplace mantel in the den.

Nissan Stock Racing Car

Illus. 143

Materials List

Hardwood Stock, ¾" .... *6" × 11"*
Hardwood Block .... *3" × 3" × 11"*
Hardwood Dowel, ¼" .... *10"*
Hardwood Toy Wheels, 1½" .... *4 each*
Carpenter's Glue .... *Small container*
Non-toxic varnish or several colors of paint in
  small containers

Cutting List

Part 1 ... *Body Center Section* ... *Make 1*
Part 2 ... *Left Body Side Section* . *Make 1*
Part 3 ... *Right Body Side Section* *Make 1*

Illus. 144   Layout of parts. Nissan Stock Racing Car.

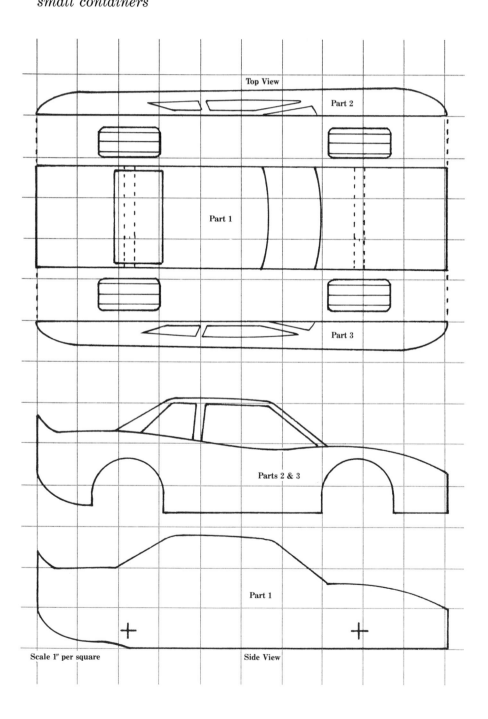

Top View

Part 2

Part 1

Part 3

Parts 2 & 3

Part 1

Scale 1" per square

Side View

Illus. 145   Completed assembly of Nissan Stock Car body.

Instructions

LAYOUT

1. Lay out the body center section (Part 1) on the hardwood block material (Illus. 144).

2. Lay out the two body side sections (Parts 2 and 3) on the ¾″ hardwood stock (Illus. 144).

3. Use a band saw or jigsaw to cut these parts to shape.

4. Shape, detail, and sand the above parts to prepare them for final assembly.

ASSEMBLY

5. Drill the axle holes through the body center section (Part 1), as indicated in Illus. 144.

6. Position the two body side sections (Parts 2 and 3) at the sides of the body center section (Part 1), and secure with carpenter's glue (Illus. 145).

7. Paint or varnish the assembly and the wheels (prior to installation of the wheels).

8. Install the four 1½″ diameter wheels and axles at this time.

9. This Nissan Stock Racing Car is now complete and ready for its first big race.

Toyota Stock Racing Car

Illus. 146

Materials List

Hardwood Stock, ¾" .... *6" × 10"*
Hardwood Block .... *3" × 3" × 10"*
Hardwood Dowel, ¼" .... *10"*
Hardwood Toy Wheels, 1½" diameter . 4 each
Carpenter's Glue .... *Small container*
*Non-toxic varnish or several colors of paint in
    small containers*

Cutting List

Part 1 ... Body Center Section ... Make 1
Part 2 ... Left Body Side Section . Make 1
*Part 3 ... Right Body Side
            Section* .... *Make 1*

*Illus. 147   Layout of
parts. Toyota Stock Rac-
ing Car.*

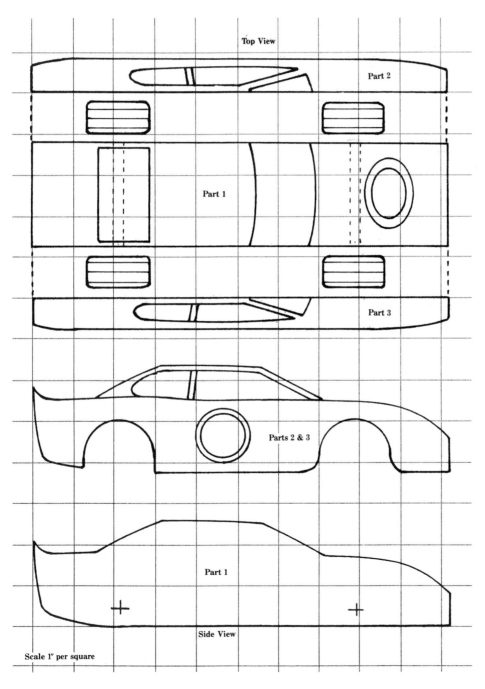

Instructions

LAYOUT

1. Lay out the body center section (Part 1) on the hardwood block material (Illus. 147).

2. Lay out the two body side sections (Parts 2 and 3) on the ¾″ hardwood stock (Illus. 147).

3. Use a band saw or jigsaw to cut these parts to shape (Illus. 148).

4. Shape, detail, and sand the above parts to prepare them for final assembly.

ASSEMBLY

5. Drill the axle holes through the body center section (Part 1), as indicated in Illus. 147.

6. Position the two body side sections (Parts 2 and 3) at the sides of the body center section (Part 1), and secure there with carpenter's glue (Illus. 149).

7. Paint or varnish the assembly and the wheels (prior to installation of the wheels).

8. Install the four 1½″ diameter wheels and axles at this time.

9. Your Toyota Stock Racing Car is now complete and ready to compete in the Daytona 500.

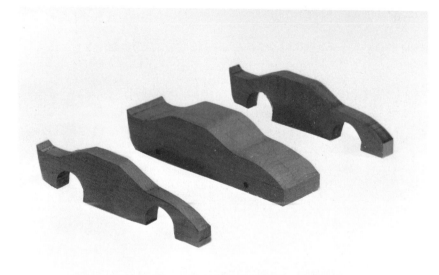

Illus. 148   Cut out these parts with your band saw.

Illus. 149   Toyota Stock Car body assembled.

· 10 ·
MORE RACING MACHINES

Car enthusiasts have learned to compete in many ways. Only a few of these have been discussed so far. Among the more specialized types of racing are drag racing and hill climbing.

Drag racing is very much like the 100-meter dash in the Summer Olympic Games, except that cars are raced instead of people. Yet it is a short, fast race on a straight track. The aim is to build a car that, beginning from a standing start, can travel approximately one-fourth of a mile (403 meters) in the shortest possible time. These cars are quite unique, with powerful engines, lightweight designs, and very long front ends to help maintain control during these tremendously fast races.

The hill climbing cars are unique, too, designed to race on dirt tracks or roads that twist and turn up the sides of mountain switchbacks. They have the power to climb at high speeds, the traction to maintain control, and the stamina to last through these grueling contests of endurance.

Either of the projects in this chapter will take a couple of afternoons to complete, painting excluded. Once again, pay attention to detail and you're going to see some great results.

Pikes Peak Racing Vehicle

Illus. 150

Materials List

Hardwood Stock, ¾" .... 2" × 6"
Hardwood Block .... 2" × 3" × 12"
Hardwood Dowel, ³/₁₆" .... 5"
Hardwood Dowel, ¼" .... 15"
Hardwood Dowel, ⁷/₁₆" .... 2"
Hardwood Toy Wheels, 1½" diameter . 2 each
Hardwood Toy Wheels, 2" diameter .. 2 each
Carpenter's Glue .... Small container
Non-toxic varnish or two or three colors of
   paint in small containers

Cutting List

Part 1 ... Body Center Section ... Make 1
Part 2 ... Left Body Side Section . Make 1
Part 3 ... Right Body Side Section Make 1
Part 4 ... Driver .... Make 1
Part 5 ... Engine Air Intake Port . Make 4
Part 6 ... Engine Oil Cooler ..... Make 1
Part 7 ... Rollbar Side Support ... Make 2

Instructions

LAYOUT

1. Lay out the body center section (Part 1) and the left and right body side sections (Parts 2 and 3) on the hardwood block material (Illus. 151).

2. Lay out the engine oil cooler (Part 6) and the two rollbar side supports (Part 7) on the ¾" hardwood stock (Illus. 151).

3. Use a band saw or jigsaw to cut these parts to shape (Illus. 152).

4. Make the driver (Part 4) from ⁷/₁₆" diameter dowel according to the instructions in Chapter 1 (Illus. 151 and 11).

5. The engine air intake ports (Part 5) are simply ¼" dowel sections cut to lengths of 1" (Illus. 151 and 152).

6. Shape, detail, and sand all of the above parts to make them ready for assembly.

ASSEMBLY

7. Drill the axle holes through the body center section (Illus. 151).

8. Drill a ¹⁵/₃₂" hole for mounting the driver (Illus. 151).

9. Drill four ¼" holes for installing the engine air intake ports (Illus. 151).

10. Position the two body side sections relative to the body center section and secure them with carpenter's glue (Illus. 151).

11. Install and glue in place the four engine air intake ports (Part 5) (Illus. 151).

12. Glue the engine oil cooler (Part 6) in place (Illus. 151).

13. Make the rollbar assembly by gluing two ³/₁₆" diameter dowel sections between the two rollbar side supports (Part 7) (Illus. 151 and 153).

14. Glue the rollbar assembly in place (Illus. 151 and 153).

15. Paint or varnish the assembly and all remaining unassembled parts.

16. Insert the driver (Part 4) in place with a bit of carpenter's glue (Illus. 151 and 153).

17. Install the 2" diameter hardwood toy wheels at the rear of the car, and the 1½" wheels at the front.

18. The Pikes Peak hill-climbing racer is now complete.

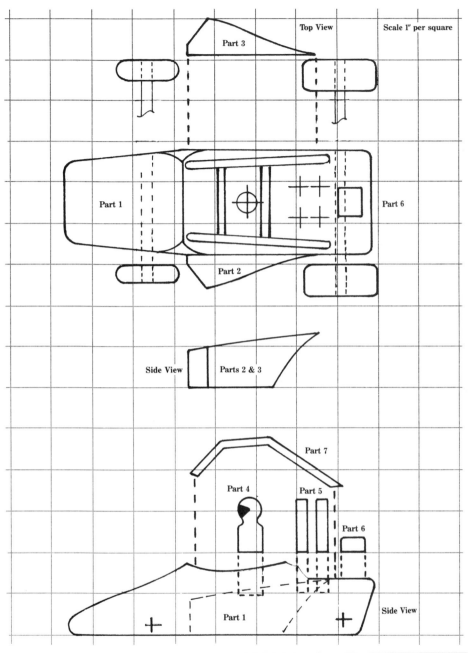

Part 3

Top View

Scale 1″ per square

Part 1

Part 6

Part 2

Side View   Parts 2 & 3

Part 7

Part 4   Part 5

Part 6

Part 1   Side View

Illus. 152   Shape, detail, and sand.

Illus. 153   Complete assembly.

Drag Racer

Illus. 154

Materials List

Hardwood Stock, ¾" .... 2" × 3"
Hardwood Block .... 1½" × 2½" × 13"
Hardwood Dowel, ¼" .... 25"
Hardwood Dowel, ⁷⁄₁₆" .... 2"
Hardwood Dowel, 1" .... 2"
Hardwood Toy Wheels, 1" diameter .. 2 each
Hardwood Toy Wheels, 2¼" diameter . 2 each
Carpenter's Glue .... Small container
Non-toxic varnish or several colors of paint in
    small containers

Cutting List

Part 1 ... Car Body .... Make 1
Part 2 ... Driver .... Make 1
Part 3 ... Driver's Headrest ...... Make 1
Part 4 ... Engine Supercharger ... Make 1
Part 5 ... Engine Header Pipe ... Make 8
Part 6 ... Folded Parachute ...... Make 1

INSTRUCTIONS

LAYOUT

1. Lay out the car body (Part 1) on the hardwood block material (Illus. 155).

2. Lay out the engine supercharger (Part 4) and the folded parachute (Part 5) on the ¾" hardwood stock material (Illus. 155).

3. Use a band saw or jigsaw to cut these parts to shape (Illus. 156).

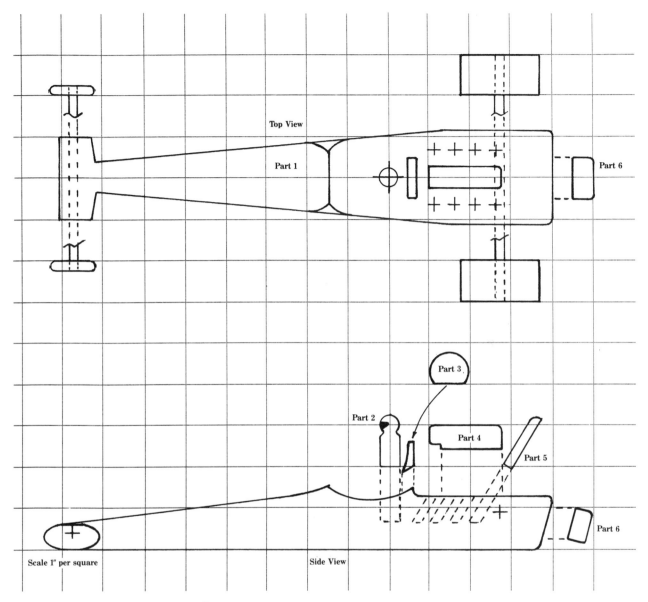

Illus. 155   Parts layout. Drag Racer.

4. The driver (Part 2) can be made from ⁷⁄₁₆″ dowel stock, according to the instructions in Chapter 1 (Illus. 155 and 11).

5. The driver's headrest is made from a portion of 1″ diameter dowel, cut and then sanded flat on one side (Illus. 155).

6. The engine header pipes are ¼″ dowel sections cut to lengths of 1½″. Each is cut at a 30° angle on one end (Illus. 155).

7. All of these parts should be shaped and detailed, as desired, and sanded in preparation for assembly.

ASSEMBLY

8. Drill the axle holes through the car body (Part 1) (Illus. 155).

9. Drill the ¹⁵⁄₃₂″ hole for the driver in the top of the car body (Part 1) (Illus. 155).

Illus. 156   Cut out these parts with your jigsaw.

Illus. 157   Dragster body assembly done.

10. Drill the eight 9/32″ holes for the engine header pipes (Illus. 155). These holes will have to be drilled with a hand-held drill motor. They should tilt towards the rear of the car at 30° angles and outwards at 10° angles. To facilitate the production of uniform holes, place a dowel in the first hole drilled and use it as a gauge for drilling the others.

11. Glue the driver's headrest (Part 3), the engine supercharger (Part 4), and the folded parachute (Part 6) in place on the car body (Part 1) (Illus. 155 and 157).

12. Insert each of the engine header pipes into the holes provided with a drop of glue.

Turn the pipe until its top is as parallel to the top of the car body as possible (Illus. 155 and 157).

13. Paint or varnish the completed assembly now, as well as the remaining unassembled parts.

14. Install the 2¼″ hardwood toy wheels at the rear and the 1″ wheels at the front of the car.

15. Insert the driver (Part 2) in its mounting hole with a drop of glue.

16. This superfast drag racing machine is now complete.

· 11 ·
OFF THE BEATEN PATH

There are those of us who are quite content to stick to well-travelled highways and byways. However, there are as well those of us who must see what that other side of the mountain looks like. For individuals of the latter group, a special type of vehicle has been developed. A vehicle of sturdy construction, designed to withstand the abuse of off-road travel, and able to shift into all-wheel drive to minimize possibilities of getting stuck. Vehicles of this type are normally equipped with special high-traction tires for maximum performance in mud and snow. They have high ground clearance and special guard plates underneath to prevent damage to their vital drive and running gear components. These vehicles are growing in popularity year by year, and some have become classics in their own right. You'll enjoy a couple of afternoons in your shop for each of these projects.

4 × 4 Toyota

Illus. 158

Materials List

Hardwood Stock, ¾" .... 5" × 20"
Hardwood Block .... 1½" × 2" × 6"
Hardwood Dowel, ⅛" .... 15"
Hardwood Dowel, ¼" .... 20"
Hardwood Toy Wheel, ¾" diameter ... 1 each
Hardwood Toy Wheels, 1½" diameter . 5 each
Carpenter's Glue .... *Small container*
*Non-toxic varnish or two or three colors of
    paint in small containers*

Cutting List

Part 1 ... *Chassis* .... *Make 1*
Part 2 ... *Engine Hood* .... *Make 1*
Part 3 ... *Rear Floor* .... *Make 1*
Part 4 ... *Right Body Side Section* *Make 1*
Part 5 ... *Left Body Side Section* . *Make 1*
Part 6 ... *Right Front Fender* .... *Make 1*
Part 7 ... *Left Front Fender* ...... *Make 1*
Part 8 ... *Right Rear Fender* ..... *Make 1*
Part 9 ... *Left Rear Fender* ...... *Make 1*
Part 10 .. *Seat* .... *Make 2*
Part 11 .. *Rollbar Assembly* ...... *Make 1*
Part 12 .. *Front Bumper* .... *Make 1*
Part 13 .. *Tailgate* .... *Make 1*

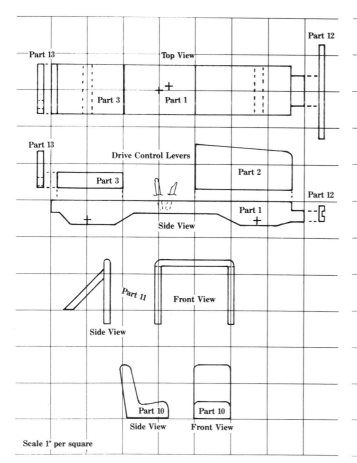

Illus. 159   Layout. 4×4 Toyota.

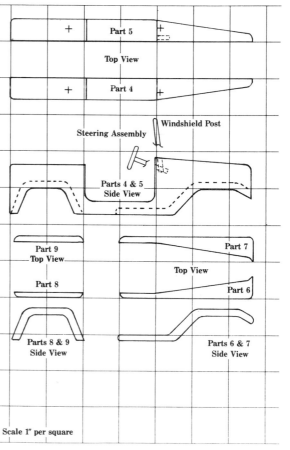

Illus. 160   Layout.

Instructions

LAYOUT

1. Lay out the chassis (Part 1), the rear floor (Part 3), the right and left body side sections (Parts 4 and 5), the right and left front fenders (Parts 6 and 7), the right and left rear fenders (Parts 8 and 9), the front bumpers (Part 12) and the tailgate (Part 13) on the ¾″ hardwood stock material (Illus. 159 and 160).

2. Lay out the engine hood (Part 2) and the two seats (Part 10) on the hardwood block material (Illus. 159).

3. Cut all of the above parts to shape using a band saw or jigsaw.

4. Shape, detail, and sand all of the above parts to prepare them for assembly.

ASSEMBLY

5. Drill the axle holes through the chassis (Part 1) (Illus. 159).

6. Position the engine hood (Part 2) and the rear floor (Part 3) on the chassis (Part 1), and secure with glue. Be sure to allow enough room behind Part 3 for the tailgate (Part 13), to be installed later (Illus. 159).

7. Align and glue in place the two body side sections (Parts 4 and 5) (Illus. 160).

8. Install the right and left front fenders (Parts 6 and 7) with carpenter's glue (Illus. 160).

9. Install the right and left rear fenders (Parts 8 and 9) in the same way (Illus. 160).

10. Drill the ⅛″ mounting holes for the windshield post, the steering column, and the gearshift and four-wheel drive control levers (Illus. 159 and 160).

11. Drill the ¼″ holes for mounting the rollbar (Illus. 160).

12. The gearshift and four-wheel control levers are made from ⅛″ dowel. Handle shapes are created with sandpaper (Illus. 159).

13. Using ⅛″ dowel sections, install the steering column, the gearshift and four-wheel drive control levers, and the windshield post (Illus. 159 and 160).

14. Complete the windshield construction by gluing a ⅛″ dowel section across the two posts and sanding the corners to form a smooth, rounded joint (Illus. 161).

15. Complete the steering assembly by gluing the ¾″ hardwood toy wheel to the end of the steering column (Illus. 160 and 161).

16. Glue the vertical rollbar posts in place, in the mounting holes.

17. Position and glue the rollbar crosspiece to the tops of the posts. You will get a better glue joint if you use a small round wood rasp to "cup" the tops of the posts a little, to have them conform with the rounded shape of the crosspiece.

18. Shape the corners of the rollbar until rounded using a wood rasp and sandpaper (Illus. 159 and 161).

19. Cut and fit the rollbar diagonal braces and glue them into position (Illus. 159 and 161).

20. Glue the front bumper (Part 12) and the tailgate (Part 13) in place, as shown (Illus. 159 and 161).

21. Drill the ¼″ spare tire mounting hole in the tailgate (Illus. 159).

22. Paint or varnish the almost completed assembly and the unassembled parts before continuing.

23. Install the five 1½″ hardwood toy wheels—the four on the ground and the spare (Illus. 161).

24. This completes the construction of the 4 × 4 Toyota.

Illus. 161   Toyota 4 × 4 after completion of assembly.

4 × 4 Pickup

Illus. 162

Materials List

Hardwood Stock, ¾" .... *6" × 15"*
Hardwood Block .... *2" × 3" × 10"*
Hardwood Dowel, ⅛" .... *5"*
Hardwood Dowel, ¼" .... *18"*
Hardwood Toy Wheels, 1½" diameter . *4 each*
Carpenter's Glue .... *Small container*
Non-toxic varnish or two or three colors of paint in small containers

Cutting List

Part 1 ... *Body Center Section* ... *Make 1*
Part 2 ... *Right Body Side Section* *Make 1*
Part 3 ... *Left Body Side Section* . *Make 1*
Part 4 ... *Truck Bed Floor* .... *Make 1*
Part 5 ... *Fender Well Body* ...... *Make 2*
Part 6 ... *Fender Well Side* .... *Make 2*
Part 7 ... *Push Guard Side* ...... *Make 2*

Instructions

LAYOUT

1. Lay out the body center section (Part 1) on the hardwood block material (Illus. 163 and 164).

2. Lay out the two body side sections (Parts 2 and 3), the truck bed floor (Part 4), the two fender well bodies (Part 5), the two fender well sides (Part 6), and the two push guard sides (Part 7) on the ¾" hardwood stock material (Illus. 163, 164, and 165).

3. Using a band saw or jigsaw, cut all of the above parts to shape (Illus. 166).

4. Prepare these parts for assembly by shaping, detailing, and sanding, as desired.

ASSEMBLY

5. Drill the axle holes through the body center section (Part 1) (Illus. 163).

6. Position the two body side sections (Parts 2 and 3) at the sides of the body center section

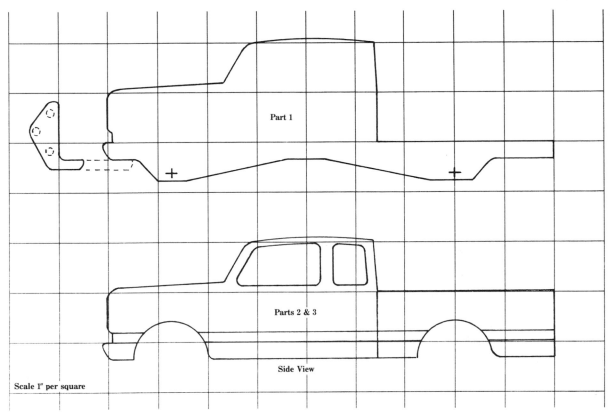

Part 1

Parts 2 & 3

Side View

Scale 1″ per square

Illus. 163   4 × 4 Pickup parts layout.

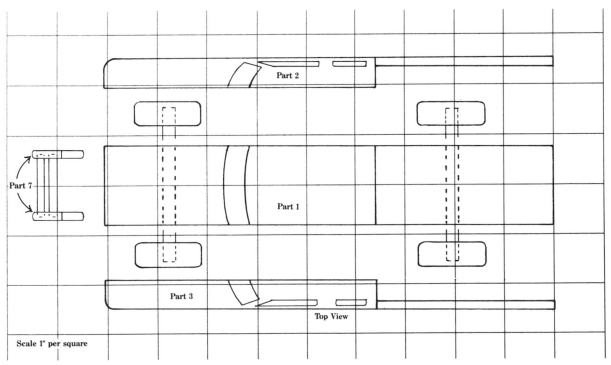

Part 2

Part 7

Part 1

Part 3

Top View

Scale 1″ per square

Illus. 164   4 × 4 Pickup parts layout.

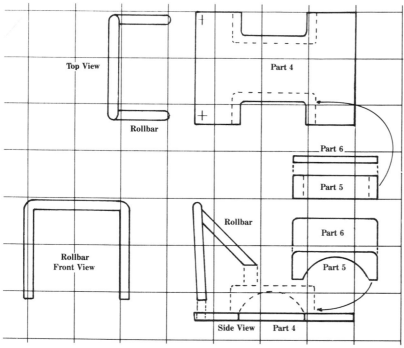

Top View

Rollbar

Part 4

Part 6

Part 5

Rollbar

Part 6

Rollbar
Front View

Part 5

Side View   Part 4

Illus. 166   Parts prepared for assembly.

(Part 1), and secure there with carpenter's glue (Illus. 164).

7. Glue the truck bed floor (Part 4) in place.

8. Install the fender well bodies (Part 5) and the fender well sides with glue.

9. Drill the ¼" holes in the truck bed floor for mounting the rollbar (Illus. 165).

10. Glue the rollbar posts in place.

11. Using a small round wood rasp, "cup" the tops of the rollbar posts so that the crossbar will fit more readily.

12. Glue the crossbar in place, and shape the corners with a rasp and sandpaper until rounded (Illus. 165).

13. Cut and fit the rollbar diagonal braces and glue them in place (Illus. 165).

14. Drill the ⅛" crossbar mounting holes into each of the push guard sides (Part 7) (Illus. 163).

15. Cut three 1" sections of ⅛" dowel and fit and glue them between the two push guard sides (Part 7), building up the push guard assembly (Illus. 163 and 164).

16. Glue the push guard assembly into place at the front of the truck.

17. Paint or varnish the entire project at this time, including the unassembled parts.

18. Install the four 1½" hardwood wheels and their associated dowel axles.

19. The 4 × 4 Pickup is completed and ready for a romp in the wild country.

· 12 ·
CARS AT WORK

The automobile has taken root in our lives in every way. It has truly become a servant of our needs. Each day, we all depend upon this marvel of modern machinery to help us carry out our errands. We have learned that we are virtually helpless without it. Something often overlooked is the fact that we have also given our motorized vehicles some fairly heavy responsibilities: we've made them sentries to our safety and well-being.

The "Highway Patrol" car here is a normal-enough-looking car, but it is actually quite specialized. The engine is a highly-tuned power plant, very similar to the ones found in the racing cars of the previous chapters. The suspension and running gear, too, are high performance components, designed for control and high speeds. Of course, the cars are always busy, maintaining the safety of highways and public streets.

The other car in this chapter is a U.S. Forest Service patrol vehicle. The rangers who use these cars have responsibilities in the mountains and forests of the United States. They often must traverse rough country to protect U.S. citizens from fire and flood, or to carry out rescue operations. They're cars of the rugged four-wheel drive variety, built to meet these tasks.

Have a good time constructing each of these classic, public service vehicles.

Highway Patrol Car

Illus. 167

Materials List

Hardwood Stock, ¾" .... *6" × 11"*
Hardwood Block .... *2" × 3" × 11"*
Hardwood Dowel, ⅛" .... *4"*
Hardwood Dowel, ¼" .... *10"*
Hardwood Dowel, 7⁄16" .... *3"*
Hardwood Toy Wheels, 1½" diameter . *4 each*
Carpenter's glue .... *Small container*
Non-toxic varnish or several colors of paint in small containers

Cutting List

Part 1 ... Body Center Section ... Make 1
Part 2 ... Right Body Side Section Make 1
Part 3 ... Left Body Side Section . Make 1
Part 4 ... Push Guard Side ...... Make 2
Part 5 ... Emergency Lights ..... Make 1

Instructions

LAYOUT

1. Lay out the body center section (Part 1) on the hardwood block material (Illus. 168 and 169).

2. Lay out the two body side sections (Parts 2 and 3) and the push guard sides (Part 4) on the ¾" hardwood material (Illus. 168 and 169).

3. Use a band saw or jigsaw to cut all of these parts to shape (Illus. 170).

4. Shape, detail, and sand these parts to prepare them for assembly.

ASSEMBLY

5. Drill the axle holes through the body center section (Part 1) (Illus. 168).

6. Position the right and left body side sections (Parts 2 and 3) at the sides of the body center section (Part 1), and secure there with carpenter's glue (Illus. 169).

7. Drill the ¼" holes for mounting the spotlights (Illus. 168 and 169).

8. Shape the spotlights from sections of ¼" dowel, and glue them into these holes (Illus. 168 and 169).

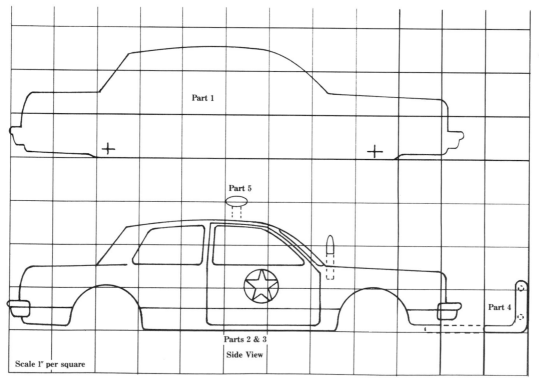

*Illus. 168
Layout of parts
for Patrol Car.*

Part 1

Part 5

Part 4

Parts 2 & 3
Side View

Scale 1" per square

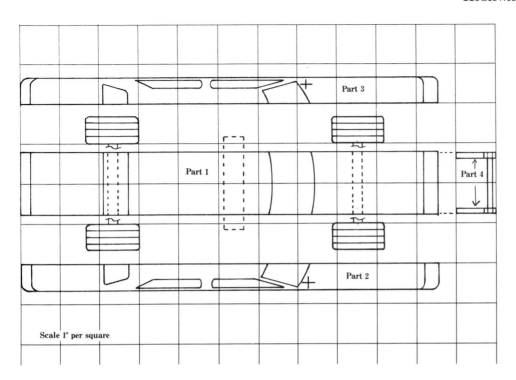

Illus. 169   Layout. Patrol Car.

Part 3

Part 1

Part 4

Part 2

Scale 1″ per square

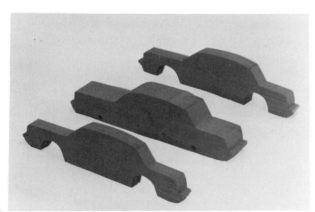

Illus. 170   The major parts for the Highway Patrol Car are cut out with a band saw.

Illus. 171   Highway Patrol Car ready for painting.

9. Sand a section of ⁷⁄₁₆″ dowel to an oval shape, to form the emergency lights (Part 5) (Illus. 168 and 169).

10. Glue the emergency lights (Part 5) in place at the top of the car assembly (Illus. 168 and 169).

11. Drill the two crossbar mounting holes into the push guard sides (Part 4) (Illus. 168).

12. Cut two sections of ⅛″ dowel to lengths of 1¼″ and glue them between the two push guard sides (Part 4), building up the push guard assembly (Illus. 168 and 169).

13. Glue the push guard assembly in place at the center and front of the car (Illus. 171).

14. Paint or varnish the almost completed assembly and all unassembled parts.

15. Install the four 1½″ hardwood toy wheels and the associated dowel axles.

16. This Highway Patrol is now complete.

U.S. Forest Ranger

Illus. 172

Materials List

Hardwood Stock, ¾" .... *6" × 9"*
Hardwood Block .... *2" × 3½" × 9"*
Hardwood Dowel, ¼" .... *10"*
Hardwood Dowel, ⁷⁄₁₆" .... *3"*
Hardwood Toy Wheels, 1½" diameter . *4 each*
Carpenter's glue .... *Small container*
Non-toxic varnish or several colors of paint in small containers

Cutting List

Part 1 ... *Body Center Section* ... *Make 1*
Part 2 ... *Right Body Side Section* *Make 1*
Part 3 ... *Left Body Side Section* . *Make 1*
Part 4 ... *Emergency Lights* ..... *Make 1*

Instructions

LAYOUT

1. Lay out the body center section (Part 1) on the hardwood block material (Illus. 173 and 174).

2. Lay out the two body side sections (Parts 2 and 3) on the ¾" hardwood material (Illus. 173 and 174).

3. Use a band saw or jigsaw to cut all of these parts to shape (Illus. 175).

4. Shape, detail, and sand these parts to prepare them for assembly.

ASSEMBLY

5. Drill the axle holes through the body center section (Part 1) (Illus. 173).

6. Position the right and left body side sections (Parts 2 and 3) at the sides of the body center section (Part 1), and secure there with carpenter's glue (Illus. 174).

7. Drill the ¼" hole for mounting the spotlight (Illus. 173 and 174).

8. Shape the spotlight from a section of ¼" dowel and glue into this hole (Illus. 173 and 174).

9. Sand a section of ⁷⁄₁₆" dowel to an oval shape, to form the emergency lights (Part 4) (Illus. 173 and 174).

10. Glue the emergency lights (Part 4) in place at the top of the car assembly (Illus. 173 and 176).

12. Paint or varnish the nearly completed assembly and all unassembled parts.

13. Install the four 1½" hardwood toy wheels and the associated dowel axles.

14. The U.S. Forest Ranger car is now complete and ready for service.

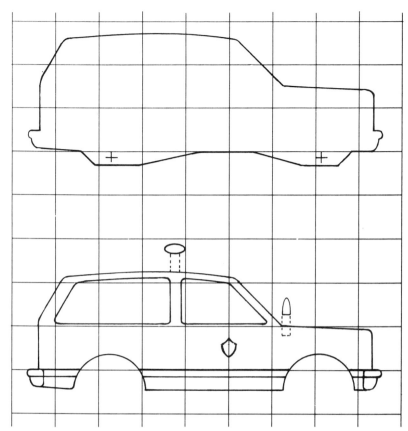

Illus. 173   Layout of parts.

Illus. 175   The three major parts for the Forest Ranger.

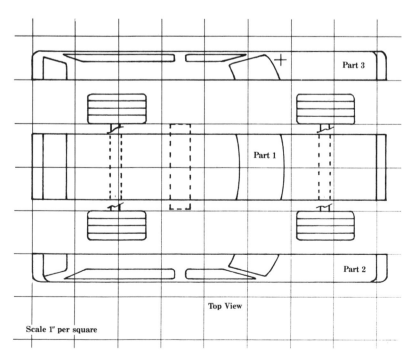

Illus. 174   Layout.

Illus. 176

· 13 ·
THE RECREATION VEHICLE

The work week is over. We now have a couple of days to relax before the grind begins all over again. Perhaps we should get away from the city—to some quiet mountain campground or serene lakeside fishing spot. Well, yes, there is a vehicle that has been created for these occasions, too. It's the recreation vehicle. It is available in a wide variety of sizes, from very small to very large. Some of these units are carried on the backs of pick-up trucks, while others have the truck built right into them. Still others are built upon trailers and are then towed behind the motor vehicle.

This chapter features one of the most recently developed types of recreation vehicles, the "fifth wheel travel trailer." It is designed to couple to a "fifth wheel"-type semi-trailer hitch, mounted above the rear axle of an open bed pickup truck. These trailers have lots of room and all the modern conveniences of home, and handle very well on the open road.

Fifth Wheel Trailer

Illus. 177

Materials List

Hardwood Stock, ¾" .... *3″ × 24″*	*Hardwood Toy Wheels, 1″ diameter* .. *4 each*
Hardwood Block .... *3″ × 15″*	*Wire Brads, ¾"* .... *Small container*
Hardwood Dowel, ⅛" .... *4″*	*Carpenter's Glue* .... *Small container*
Hardwood Dowel, ¼" .... *10″*	*Non-toxic varnish or two or three colors of*
Plywood, ¼" thickness .... *10″ × 18″*	*paint in small containers*

Cutting List

Part 1 ... *Body Side Wall* .... Make 2
Part 2 ... *Main Chassis* .... Make 1
Part 3 ... *Body Roof* .... Make 1
Part 4 ... *Rear Wall* .... Make 1
Part 5 ... *Lower Forward Wall* ... Make 1
Part 6 ... *Upper Forward Chassis* Make 1

Part 7 ... *Forward Wall* .... Make 1
Part 8 ... *Hitch Mount* .... Make 1
Part 9 ... *Large Roof Vent* ...... Make 1
Part 10 .. *Small Roof Vent* ...... Make 2
Part 11 .. *Parking Jacks* .... Make 2
Part 12 .. *Trailer Hitch* .... Make 1

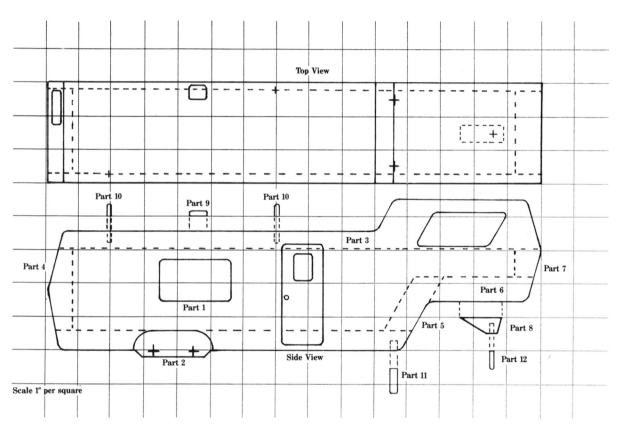

Illus. 178 Layout of parts. Fifth Wheel Trailer.

Instructions

LAYOUT

1. Lay out the two body side walls (Part 1) on ¼"-thick, good grade plywood material (Illus. 178).

2. Lay out the main chassis (Part 2), the rear wall (Part 4), the lower forward wall (Part 5), the upper forward chassis (Part 6), the forward wall (Part 7), the hitch mount (Part 8), and the large roof vent (Part 9) on ¾" hardwood stock material (Illus. 178).

3. Lay out the body roof (Part 3) on the hardwood block material (Illus. 178).

4. Make the parking jacks (Part 11) from sections of ¼" hardwood dowel.

5. The small roof vents (Part 10) and the

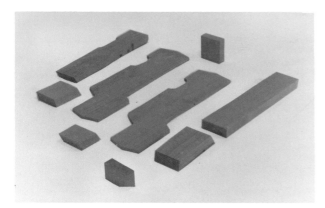

Illus. 179   Cut out with band saw or jigsaw.

Illus. 180   Complete assembly of the Fifth Wheel Trailer.

trailer hitch (Part 12) are to be made from ⅛″ dowel stock (Illus. 178).

6. You may use your band saw, jigsaw, table saw, and/or radial arm saw to cut all of the parts to shape (Illus. 179).

7. Shape, detail, and sand all parts, as you desire, to prepare them for final assembly.

ASSEMBLY

8. Drill the axle holes through the main chassis (Part 2) (Illus. 178).

9. Drill ⅛″ holes for installing the trailer hitch (Part 12) and the two small roof vents (Part 10), at the locations indicated in Illus. 178.

10. Drill two ¼″ holes for installing the parking jacks (Part 11) in the bottom of the main chassis (Part 2), as shown in the drawing (Illus. 178).

11. Place the main chassis (Part 2) on edge on your workbench. Position one of the body side walls (Part 1) over the main chassis. Secure these parts together with carpenter's glue and wire brads.

12. Now position the rear wall (Part 4) and secure in the same way.

13. Do the same with Parts 5, 6, 7, and 3, in that order.

14. Turn the assembly over, and attach the opposite body side wall (Part 1) in a like manner, being careful to maintain proper alignment as you work.

15. The finish sanding and shaping of the assembly should be done at this time.

16. Install the hitch mount (Part 8), the trailer hitch (Part 12), the parking jacks (Part 11), and the roof vents (Parts 9 and 10) with carpenter's glue (Illus. 178).

17. Varnish or paint all parts.

18. Install the 1″ diameter hardwood wheels and axles (Illus. 178 and 180).

19. This completes the assembly of your Fifth Wheel Recreation Vehicle. Go on now to make the truck for towing it.

Towing Vehicle

Materials List

Hardwood Stock, ¾" .... 5" × 10"
Hardwood Block .... 1½" × 2½" × 8"
Hardwood Dowel, ¼" .... 8"
Hardwood Toy Wheels, 1" diameter .. 4 each
Carpenter's Glue .... Small container
Non-toxic varnish or paint in two or three colors in small containers

Cutting List

Part 1 ... Body Center Section ... Make 1
Part 2 ... Right Body Side Section Make 1
Part 3 ... Left Body Side Section . Make 1
Part 4 ... Trailer Hitch Cross
                    Mount .... Make 1
Part 5 ... Fifth Wheel .... Make 1
Part 6 ... Tail Gate .... Make 1

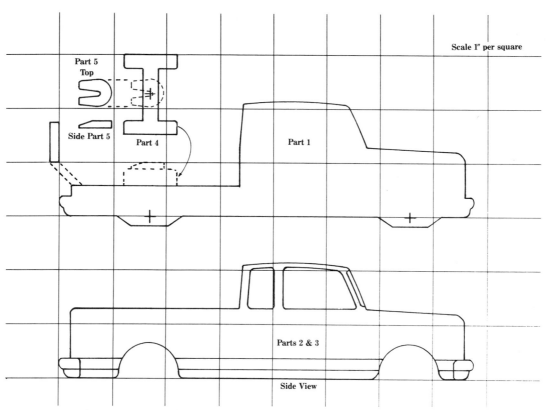

Illus. 181   Layout of parts for the Towing Vehicle.

Instructions

LAYOUT

1. Lay out the body center section (Part 1) on the hardwood block material (Illus. 181 and 182).

2. Lay out the two body side sections (Parts 2 and 3), the trailer hitch cross mount (Part 4), the fifth wheel (Part 5), and the tailgate (Part 6) on the ¾" hardwood stock (Illus. 181 and 182).

3. Use your band saw or jigsaw to cut all of the parts to shape (Illus. 183).

4. Shape, detail, and sand all of these parts to prepare them for final assembly.

ASSEMBLY

5. Drill the two axle holes through the body center section (Part 1) (Illus. 181).

6. Position the two body side sections (Parts 2 and 3) at the sides of the body center section (Part 1) and secure there with carpenter's glue.

7. Glue the trailer hitch cross mount (Part 4) in position directly over the rear axle area in the truck bed (Illus. 181).

8. Drill the ⅛″ hole in the center of the trailer hitch cross mount (Part 4) (Illus. 181).

9. Place the fifth wheel (Part 5) on the trailer hitch cross mount (Part 4) in such a way that it is centered and does not block the hole drilled in step 8 (Illus. 181).

10. Glue the tailgate (Part 6) in place.

11. Paint or varnish the assembly and all unassembled parts at this time.

12. Install the four 1″ diameter wheels and the required axles.

13. Your towing vehicle is now finished and ready for use with your fifth wheel trailer.

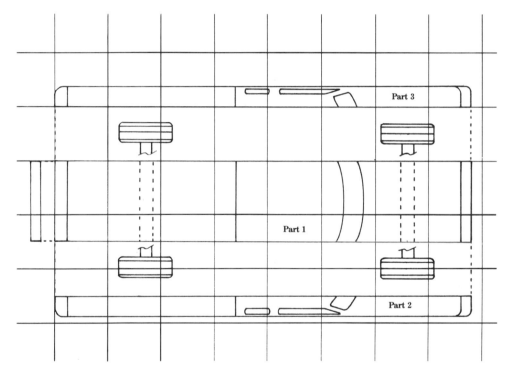

Illus. 182   Layout of parts for the Towing Vehicle.

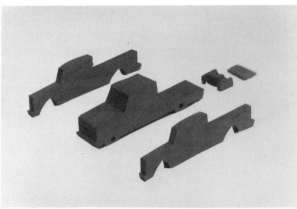

Illus. 183   Prepare for assembly.

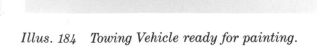

Illus. 184   Towing Vehicle ready for painting.

METRIC CONVERSION

MM—MILLIMETRES   CM—CENTIMETRES

INCHES TO MILLIMETRES AND CENTIMETRES

INCHES	MM	CM	INCHES	CM	INCHES	CM
1/8	3	0.3	9	22.9	30	76.2
1/4	6	0.6	10	25.4	31	78.7
3/8	10	1.0	11	27.9	32	81.3
1/2	13	1.3	12	30.5	33	83.8
5/8	16	1.6	13	33.0	34	86.4
3/4	19	1.9	14	35.6	35	88.9
7/8	22	2.2	15	38.1	36	91.4
1	25	2.5	16	40.6	37	94.0
1 1/4	32	3.2	17	43.2	38	96.5
1 1/2	38	3.8	18	45.7	39	99.1
1 3/4	44	4.4	19	48.3	40	101.6
2	51	5.1	20	50.8	41	104.1
2 1/2	64	6.4	21	53.3	42	106.7
3	76	7.6	22	55.9	43	109.2
3 1/2	89	8.9	23	58.4	44	111.8
4	102	10.2	24	61.0	45	114.3
4 1/2	114	11.4	25	63.5	46	116.8
5	127	12.7	26	66.0	47	119.4
6	152	15.2	27	68.6	48	121.9
7	178	17.8	28	71.1	49	124.5
8	203	20.3	29	73.7	50	127.0

INDEX